Japan Travel Guide

Things I Wish I Knew Before Going To Japan

By Ken Fukuyama & Yuki Fukuyama

Table of Contents

Introduction 1

Chapter 1: Japan's Magic..3

   Japanese People 5

   Japan Travel Highlights.. 6

Chapter 2: Wonders of Japan1 11

   Natural Wonders.. 11

      Mount Fuji 11

      Fuji Five Lakes 15

      Shiraito Falls.. 24

      Mount Yari...25

      Mount Aso 26

      Kerama Islands.. 28

   Japan's Best Kept Secrets 30

      Narai-Juku... 30

      Takaragawa Onsen Osenkaku 33

      Wakayama 35

      Nachi Falls 37

Chapter 3 - Tokyo: Where the Old Meets New 39

   Shopping in Tokyo 41

      Ginza.. 42

      Harajuku.. 44

      Shibuya Crossing.. 46

      Shinjuku 48

      Tokyo Tower 49

   Places to Visit in Tokyo 51

      Sensoji Temple 51

      Tokyo Skytree 53

      Tsukiji Fish Market 58

      Meiji Shrine 60

Tokyo Disneyland 62

Tokyo Disneysea 65

Imperial Palace and East Garden 68

Ghibli Museum 70

Akihabara 72

Sumo at Ryoguku Kokugikan 75

Tokyo National Museum 77

Jimbocho 78

What to Eat in Tokyo 79

Where to Stay in Tokyo 81

Chapter 4 - Kyoto: Home of More Than A Thousand Temples 83

Places to Visit in Kyoto 84

Kiyomizu-dera Temple 84

Nishiki Market 87

Fushimi-Inari-Taisha Shrine 89

Arashiyama Bamboo Grove 92

Kinkaku-ji Temple 94

Nijo Castle 96

Ginkaku-ji (The Silver Pavillion) 98

Amanoshashidate 100

Ryoan-ji 102

Gion 104

Kyoto Food Guide 106

Kyoto Accommodation Guide 113

Chapter 5 - Osaka: Bright Osaka Lights and Magic 115

Top Tourist Spots in Osaka 116

Osaka Castle 116

Universal Studios Japan 120

Dotonbori 123

What to Eat in Osaka 128

Where to Stay in Osaka 132

Side Trip: The Deer Paradise Called Nara 134

    Nara Deer Park 135

    Kasuga-taisha Shrine 137

    Todaiji Temple 138

    Yoshikien 140

Chapter 6 - Hokkaido: The Land of Beer, Music Boxes, and Colorful Landscapes 143

Places to See in Hokkaido 144

    Sapporo 144

    Otaru 158

    Furano-Biei 162

Where to Stay in Hokkaido 173

What to Eat in Hokkaido 176

Chapter 7 - Winter Destinations 178

Shirakawago 178

Zao Snow Monsters 180

Jigokudani Monkey Park 182

Sapporo Snow Festival 184

Otaru Snow Light Path 185

Chapter 8 - Kyushu: The Land of Fire 186

Fukuoka 187

Dazaifu 189

Kurokawa Onsen 191

Saga Pottery 192

Takachiho Gorge 195

Suizenji Gaden 197

Nagasaki 199

Amakusa 205

Sakurajima 210

Yakushima 212

Chapter 9 - The Ultimate Japan Itineraries 214

The Ultimate 7 Day Itinerary 215

The Extended Version: 10-Day Itinerary 218

7 Days in Tokyo and Hokkaido 219

3 Days in Tokyo for Food Hunters 222

5 Days in Kyushu 225

Chapter 10 - 50 Japan Travel and Budget Tips 227

Japan's Secrets and Weirdness: What's So Special About
Japan? 230

Conclusion 236

Maps & Resources 237

Introduction

Japan is one of the most fascinating countries in the whole world. It's the land of the geishas, robots, Pokémon, ninjas, samurais, and anime. It's also the home of some beautiful temples and natural wonders. You should definitely visit Japan at least once in your lifetime.

Japan is interesting to say the least. It was once a battlefield, but it's now the land of all things Kawaii. This country also has the best customer service anyone could ask for. Waiters and service crews are not motivated by tips. They treat their job as if it's their life mission.

I have worked as a tour guide in Japan for thirty years and I'll share everything I know in this book.

In this book, you'll learn about:

- ✓ The Japanese culture
- ✓ Japanese architecture and history
- ✓ Best cities to visit in Japan
- ✓ The best tourist spots
- ✓ Japan's hidden and least known gems
- ✓ The best times to visit a certain area
- ✓ Japan's winter destinations
- ✓ The best natural wonders in Japan
- ✓ Japan trip hacks
- ✓ How to travel around Japan on a budget
- ✓ Itineraries

- ✓ Where to stay

- ✓ Best tourist spots to visit

- ✓ What not to miss

- ✓ Budget tips

- ✓ The ultimate 7-day Japan itinerary

- ✓ 50 travel tips

- ✓ 71 things that make Japan special

- ✓ And more!

This book will help you understand Japanese culture, architecture, customs, and a little bit of its history. This book also contains stunning images that will make you want to fly to Japan right away.

Consider this book your very own comprehensive guide that will help you make sure that your trip to Japan is fun and hassle-free.

Chapter 1: Japan's Magic

Japan is one of the most beautiful countries in the world. Its landscapes are awe-inspiring, captivating, and intriguing. The cities are busy, noisy, and colorful. On the other hand, its countrysides are quiet, calming and peaceful, the perfect escape from the hustle and bustle of the country's urban jungles.

Its streets are lined with cherry trees that look spectacular during spring time. The country is also home to thousands of skyscrapers and hundreds of preserved traditional Japanese wooden buildings.

The Japanese archipelago is located in Asia and it's close to South Korea, North Korea, the Philippines, and Taiwan. It covers more than three hundred and sixty-four thousand kilometers of land. It became a distinct country in 1590. An archipelago means that it is made of thousands of islands. But, only four hundred and thirty islands are inhabited. Its four major islands are Honshu, Hokkaido, Shikoku, and Kyushu.

Japanese People

One of the best things about Japan is its people. If there's one word to describe Japanese people, it's disciplined. They are also polite, punctual, hard-working, respectful, and honest. You could leave your bike on the sidewalk without a chain, and it would still be there at the end of the day.

Japan Travel Highlights

There are a number of Japan cultural highlights that would make your trip to Japan memorable, including:

Tea Ceremony or Chanoyu

Matcha or powdered green tea is very much a part of the Japanese culture. The presentation of Matcha to guests in a formal tea ceremony is a sign of respect and generosity.

Kabuki

Kabuki is the traditional Japanese performing arts. Men performers usually wear makeup and play female roles.

Ikebana

Ikebana is the ancient Japanese art of flower arrangement. It uses a wide variety of flowers, flowering trees, and bonsais. Ikebana arrangements are classy and elegant.

Fabulous Origami Decor

Origami is the Japanese art of paper folding. Colorful papers are folded to form different shapes – flowers, birds, frogs, stars, and even Pokémon. According to the legend, if you fold one thousand paper cranes, your wish will be granted.

Ryokan

Ryokans are traditional Japanese inns. These inns usually have a communal bath and tatami floors. They also serve local food. If you want to know how it feels like to stay in a traditional Japanese house, you should stay in a Ryokan.

Geishas

Geishas are beautiful women who wear thick makeup and colorful clothes. They play beautiful music and dance gracefully. They are elegant and their captivating eyes hold thousands of secrets. Geishas are, no doubt, a huge part of the Japanese culture.

Manga

Manga or comic books are very much part of the modern Japanese culture. They tell interesting stories. It usually has romantic and futuristic themes and most stories involve samurais and robots.

Anime and Kawaii

Anime is basically an animated manga. Although kids enjoy anime films, these cartoons usually have adult themes and complex plots – think Samurai X. The Kawaii culture that's associated with cute cartoon characters (like Hello Kitty) is also prevalent in Japan.

Chapter 2 - Wonders of Japan

Natural Wonders

Japan is filled to the brim with breathtaking natural wonders. Here's a list of the natural wonders that you should see when you're in Japan.

Mount Fuji

Mount Fuji is well-known as the tallest mountain in Japan. Locally known as *Fujisan*, it is located at Honshu Island. The mountain is surrounded by three cities – Fujinomiya, Fujiyoshida, and Gotemba. There are five lakes around the mountain – Lake Shoji, Lake Yamanaka, Lake Sai, Lake Motosu, and Lake Kawaguchi.

You don't have to climb Mt. Fuji, but you definitely have to see it and the best way to devour the beauty of Mt. Fuji is by visiting the Fuji Five Lakes, which we will be covering in the next destination.

❖ How to get there:

One of the best things about this natural wonder is that it's situated just two hours away from Tokyo. You can take a bus at the Shinjuku Expressway Bus Terminal to reach the Fuji Subaru Line Fifth Station (alternatively known as Kawaguchi-ko Fifth Station or Yoshidaguchi Fifth Station). This is the starting point of most Mt. Fuji hikes.

❖ The best time to visit Mount Fuji:

July to September

It is also known as the Fuji hiking season. During autumn, the mountain is surrounded by colorful flowers and leaves. You can get the most stunning view. The mountain will be closed for hiking during the winter season.

❖ Entrance fee:

1000 yen or about $10.

❖ The best time to start your climb:

Around 6 to 8 am

It takes at least three hours to complete a trail. If you wish to enjoy the sunrise, make sure you start at night. Don't worry as there will still be people around even though it's dark. Viewing the sunrise from Mt. Fuji's peak is a breathtaking experience that you should not miss.

❖ Things that you should know before your climb:

a) There are four trails for you to choose from when it comes to Mount Fuji hiking.

- Yoshida Trail (5 to 8 hours): This is the most popular route. You can get a beautiful view of the Fuji Five Lakes at the beginning.

- Subashiri Trail: This trail consists of both forest and mountain routes. It starts from all the way down at the base forest of Mount Fuji.

- Gotemba Trail (8 to 10hours): This is the most time-consuming trail. It is also considered to be tougher compared to the rest. Experienced hikers who seek for more adventure can try out this trail.

- Fujinomiya Trail (4 to 7 hours): This is the shortest trail among the four. Keep in mind that the shortest trail is also said to be the steepest one.

b) Mount Fuji is divided into 10 separate rest stations.

c) Beware of altitude sickness. It can be quite common when climbing up extreme elevations.

Symptoms of altitude sickness include:

- Dizziness

- Headaches

- Breathing trouble

- Nausea

  Prevention:

- Stop and rest every 20 minutes. You can increase the climbing time after getting used to the elevation changes.

- Buy some compressed oxygen cans before you start your hike at the 5th Station. They can really help with dizziness and shortness of breath.

- There are sleeping cabins available along the trail if you decide to take a nap. Make sure to reserve them a few days ahead of your trip because they are usually full. It costs 6000 yen per cabin.

d) You need to pay 200 yen or $2 for the restrooms on Mount Fuji. The higher the restroom is, the higher the cost. So, make sure that you bring along plenty of coins.

e) You can send postcards from the peak!

The summit of Fuji is full of excitement. It's a reward for your outstanding effort to successfully reach the top. At the peak, you can find the Kusushi and Okumiya shrines, restaurants, gift shops, and more. The best part is you get to send postcards to your friends and your loved ones through the post office located at the peak.

f) What to pack?

- Hiking boots – Fuji's terrain is definitely not a bed of roses. There are lots of rocks and uneven grounds that could trip you anytime if you are not careful.

- Warm clothing – It is scorching hot at the base of Mount Fuji but don't let this trick you into wearing thin clothes. Starting from the 7th station, everything will get unbearably cold. Snow starts to fall at the peak especially during the night and early morning. It's summer at the bottom, winter at the top.

- Flashlights – If you plan to climb Mount Fuji at night, be sure to bring along a flashlight with you. It gets really dangerous if you can't even see your next step. For your convenience, you can wear flashlight helmets or headbands.

- Water – Bring the right amount of water. It gets very dry at the top, so you don't want to faint half way because of dehydration or stumble down because of the unbearable weight. Just bring around 2L and you will be just fine.

- Snacks – Pack according to your plans. Bring more food if you decide to stop and spend the night. There are hardly any restaurants around until you reach the peak. Keep in mind that there are no trash cans either along the trail.

- (Optional) Walking sticks – They are available for sale at the 5th station if you ever need one. You can get imprints on your stick as well once you have reached a specific checkpoint. It costs a few hundred yen for each of the imprints.

The Fuji Five Lakes

The lakes at the base of Mount Fuji are great natural wonders too. The areas around the lakes are covered with beautiful pink moss during the springtime. The gorgeous scenery looks like it was directly taken out of a postcard.

Yamanaka-ko is the easternmost lake, followed by Kawaguchi-ko, Sai-ko, Shoji-ko and Motosu-ko.

❖ The best time to visit the lakes:

April to May, September to November

Every year, the Fuji Shibazakura Festival is held at about three kilometers south of Motosu-ko, offering amazing views of vast fields of *shibazakura* (pink moss) with Mount Fuji as the backdrop. You would be able to see delightful fields of pink, white and purple flowers in all sorts of different hues. There are also stalls that sell pots of pink moss, souvenirs, food and local produce.

The festival is usually held from mid-April through early June. The festival was held from April 14 to May 27 in 2018. It is advisable to visit early in the mornings to avoid crowds and for good visibility.

During autumn, the lakes make a good overnight trip away from Tokyo for some leisurely strolling, while enjoying the autumn *koyo* (foliage), lake activities and hiking in the nearby mountains.

❖ How to get there:

You can get there by train, bus or even a taxi.

The cheapest way to get there is by bus.

a) Take a bus at Shinjuku Expressway Bus Terminal, which is at the opposite side of the Shinjuku Station.

b) Show your pre-booked bus ticket at the counter and they will tell you your bus platform number. The travel time is approximately 1 hour and 45 minutes.

❖ Entrance fee:

Adults: 1,750 yen, Children: 880 yen

Bonus Tip: Make sure you book your tickets a few weeks before your trip. You most probably won't be able to purchase a ticket on your departure day because it's always full especially during the holiday seasons. So, why risk it? You can pre-book at https://highway-buses.jp/

c) Once you arrived at Kawaguchiko Station, you may want to buy the one-day or two-day sightseeing bus pass rather than paying your fares at every single station. It's very much worth the money. There are three bus routes, red, green and blue. For more information, you can refer to http://bus-en.fujikyu.co.jp/heritage-tour/detail/id/1/

d) If you don't have plans to check in your accommodation first, you can store your luggage in the lockers provided. You can try going to the shops beside the station for more lockers at a cheaper price.

e) Here are some of the top destinations that you may want to visit.

- Red Line:

11 Pleasure Cruiser Ropeway Entrance.

15 Kozantei Ubuya. The 5th best stop for Mount Fuji photo shooting.

17 Kawaguchiko Music Forest Museum. An admission fee of 1500Yen is required. You may want to skip this place during the winter season.

22 Kawaguchiko Natural Living Center. The 4th best stop for Mount Fuji photo shooting. There are beautiful gardens with lots of colourful flowers.

- Green Line:

67 Nenba Minshuku. The 1st best stop for Mount Fuji photo shooting.

71 Fugaku Fuketsu (Wind Cave). You can experience the peaceful forest by taking the forest trail to the lava cave.

72 Ryugu Doketsu (Lava Cave).

- Blue Line:

71 Fugaku Fuketsu (Wind Cave). You can experience the peaceful forest by taking the forest trail to the lava cave.

72 Ryugu Doketsu (Lava Cave).

119 Kodaki Fuji View Point. The 2nd best stop for Mount Fuji photo shooting.

26 Koanso. The 3rd best stop for Mount Fuji photo shooting. There will be no buses available to this stop. It's approximately 4km from Tourist Motosuko.

Bonus Tips:

❖ If you have bought the one-day or two-day travel pass, you can ignore the price mentioned at each of the stops.

❖ Along the blue and green line, you will pass through the infamous suicide forest (Aokigahara Forest).

❖ If you would like to get off at any bus station, you will have to press the stop button found inside the bus.

What to eat in Fuji Five Lakes

#1 Hoto Fudo

It is located right in front of Kawaguchiko Station. This place is all about its special Hoto Fudo noodles with miso and pumpkin soup. You can only find this in this Fuji area and it is exceptionally good! This place is usually crowded during lunch and dinner time so you should go there either early or late if you would like to avoid the crowd. It costs about 1000 yen for one big bowl of noodles. You can request for extra bowls if you would like to share.

#2 Fuji Tempura Idaten

It is located a five-minute walk away from Kawaguchiko Station. It offers super fresh and well-cooked tempura. This place is also usually crowded. You may have to wait up to an hour. Also, the price of the food here is slightly more expensive than the other restaurants.

#3 Tetsuyaki

It is located just beside Fuji Tempura Idaten. You can find various types of food here, ranging from rice and noodles to teppanyaki. You name it, they have it. Dining here would be a great value for money!

Where to stay in Fuji Five Lakes

Since Kawaguchi-ko is the hub of the region, it has the greatest number of accommodation options. Fuji-Yoshida has a couple of good, inexpensive hostels.

If you wish to find cheaper accommodation, look for places that are further from the station. The further they are, the cheaper they get. Most inns far from the station offer free pick-up services prior to advance notice.

Please take note that if you stay at somewhere around Yamanaka-ko, you may need to pay an additional bus fare of 750 yen to get from Kawaguchiko Station to Yamanaka-ko.

All accommodations located around the red, green and blue lines are free from transportation fees if you have already purchased the sightseeing bus pass.

#1 Kozantei Ubuya

When it comes to luxury, this is the best hotel. It costs $595 per night. The hotel offers private Onsen or a hot bath with a direct view of Mount Fuji.

#2 K's House Mt Fuji

It provides spacious Japanese-style rooms at a budget-friendly price. There are common areas to meet the other tourists and mountain bikes for rent as well. Free pick-up from Kawaguchi-ko Station is available too.

#3 Kawaguchi-ko Station Inn

This famous hostel across the Kawaguchi-ko Station is spick-and-span. It offers mixed dorms with an 11.30pm curfew. Some dorms do have Fuji views and there is a top-floor bath looking out to Mount Fuji. This budget-friendly accommodation has English-speaking staff and laundry facilities as well.

Shiraito Falls – Mount Fuji Side Trip

The Shiraito Falls is located at the foot of Mount Fuji. This horseshoe-shaped waterfall is well known as the most beautiful waterfall in Japan. The water flows from a 20-meter cliff and looks like silk threads from afar. This waterfall is surrounded by trees and you can view it from a bridge near Mount Fuji.

There are quite a lot of shops selling food and souvenirs on the way down to the falls. This place is famous for its milk products, so don't forget to taste the ice-cream here.

❖   How to get there:

Take a bus from either the Shin-Fuji Station or the Fujinomiya Station.

❖   Entrance fee and opening hours:

There's no admission fee and it's open 24 hours.

Mount Yari

Mount Yari is one of the most popular mountains in Japan. It's part of the Northern Alps (Hida Mountains). It's a haven for adventurers and mountain climbers. In winter you can ski here, in summer you can enjoy the alpine plants, and in autumn you can see the red foliage.

❖ When to visit:

It's best to visit the mountains in Japan between May and November.

❖ How to get there:

Getting to this paradise is surprisingly easy. You can take direct night buses from Osaka or Tokyo.

❖ Entrance fee and opening hours:

There's no admission fee. It would be a good idea to start your hike early in the morning.

Mount Aso

This mountain is one of Japan's most well-kept secrets. It is one of the biggest volcanoes in the world and it is located on the beautiful island of Kyushu. This beautiful volcano has inspired many prized paintings and poetry. It looks intimidating and might even inspire you with its beauty.

You could also visit the Aso Volcano Museum, which provides explanations about the volcano.

❖ How to get there:

1. You can get to Mount Aso by riding a train from Kumamoto. This takes about one hour and forty minutes.

2. You can also take a three-hour bus ride from Beppu.

3. To reach the Nakadake crater, you can take a 30-minute bus ride from Aso Station.

- Entrance fee and opening hours for Mount Aso:

There's no admission fee and it's open 24 hours.

- Entrance fee and opening hours for Aso Volcano Museum:

860 yen - 9a.m. to 5p.m.

- Things that you should know before you go there:

a) If you enjoy cycling, you can rent a bicycle at Aso Station and cycle to Mount Aso.

b) As the mountain is an active volcano, make sure to check the volcano's current state before traveling there. The crater area may be closed due to heightened volcano activities.

c) Gases can be intense when you go near the area around the summit. Thus, those with respiratory problems should refrain from approaching the crater. Just in case, you can bring a face mask to reduce the smell of sulfur.

d) If you want to experience horse riding, you could go to Kusasenri, which is a plain near to the crater. Take note that horse riding is only available from early March to mid-December.

The Kerama Islands

The Kerama Islands are in Okinawa. They are one of the least known natural gems of Japan. They are a group of twenty-two islands, but only four islands are inhabited. The islands are surrounded by crystal blue waters and powder white sand. If you love diving, you should not miss visiting this place.

❖ How to get there:

You can get to the Kerama Islands by taking a speedboat from Naha. The trip takes about thirty-five minutes. You can cross from one island to another via village ferries.

❖ Things that you should know before you go there:

a) You can get your ticket from one of the diving clubs and go for a dive there without knowing how to swim. It is a good place to start for those who want to try out diving as a guide will accompany them.

b) Bring a swimsuit. You can also rent a diving suit in the area.

c) Bring medicine for seasickness if you are not used to traveling by ferries and boats.

d) Bring sunscreen. Okinawa is pretty hot during the summer time.

e) Stay hydrated. Drinks lots of water and relax in the shade.

f) July to September is typhoon season. Boats are often canceled. Do check the ferry and boat schedule before you go.

❖ Entrance fee and opening hours:

The entrance fee to the islands is free. You can visit the islands anytime, but it would be best to check the ever-changing ferry schedules before you travel. Usually, the ferries travel to and from the islands only until 5 pm. For more information, check the websites below:

http://www.vill.tokashiki.okinawa.jp/

http://www.vill.zamami.okinawa.jp/info/pricelist.html

Japan's Best Kept Secrets

As popular as it is, Japan is filled with quaint little places that manage to captivate your heart. Here are some of the spots that are less famous but will still allow you to have a fulfilling journey.

Narai-Juku

Narai-Juku is a peaceful little town in Shiojiri, Nagano Prefecture. This elevated town is in between Tokyo and Kyoto and at the foot of the Torii Mountain Pass. The city is filled with public baths and traditional inns called ryokan. Narai-juku is also known as the "Narai of One Thousand Buildings".

This beautiful town transports you to a different time. The narrow streets are lined with beautiful wooden houses. Narai-juku is the home of many historic sites, such as the simple Shizume Shrine, the Nakaruma House, Two Hundred Juzos (small Buddhist statues), Honjinato Ruins, and a 300-year-old Kiso-ohashi.

This town is as charming as it is breathtakingly beautiful. It has sort of an old town charm to it.

❖ How to get there:

To get to Narai-Juku, go to the Tokyo Shinjuku station and catch a train to Shiojiri Station. Narai is the fifth station. The trip takes about two and a half hours.

❖ When to go there:

Narai-Juku Ice Candle Festival is held annually from Feb 2 to Feb 4. You would be able to see a street full of ice candles. The glowing street is about 2 kilometers long, warmly lighting up the old port town of Kisofukushima. Visitors will feel the welcoming message of local citizens.

❖ Things that you should know before you go there:

a) The train station is at the farthest end of the road. Be sure to allocate ample time to get to your train, or you may have to wait for another hour to catch the next train as the trains are not so frequent here.

b) You may leave your luggage at the tourist center with a small fee so that you can explore the town with less burden.

Takaragawa Onsen Osenkaku

Japan is known for its hot spring public baths called onsen. These baths usually contain calcium chloride, sulfate ions, and sodium chloride. The water has a moisturizing effect that makes the skin look younger and more glowing. It can also cure various skin diseases such as eczema, heat rash, burns, atopic dermatitis, and abrasions.

However, most onsens are crowded, especially during the summertime. If you want to avoid the crowd of tourists and health buffs, head to Takaragawa Onsen Osenkaku.

Takaragawa Onsen Osenkaku is a luxurious hotel located next to the bus stop in Fujiwara, Minakami-machi. It's about a thirty-minute drive from Minakami Station.

This hotel exudes a warm and lush feel to it. The hot spring there is also excellent. It costs around $136 per night and is open from 9 am to 5 pm.

❖ How to get there:

Take a train to Minakami station. At the station, take a Kan'etsu Bus for Yunokoya and get off at Takaragawa Onsen Osenkaku.

❖ Things that you should know before you go there:

a) There are scheduled mini buses to pick you up at the station. Make sure to be punctual though.

b) There is almost nothing to do on the property beyond the onsen. A one-night stay is recommended if you only aim for the onsen experience.

c) Make sure to catch a sunset or sunrise view from the onsen overlooking the valley!

Wakayama

Wakayama is also one of Japan's rare jewels, at least compared to Tokyo and Kyoto. The city is known as the spiritual center of Japan. It has a cool and refreshing vibe that soothes every inch of your soul.

Wakayama is the home of the Komano Kodo Pilgrimage route, which is a network of trails that lead to various sacred spots such as Kumano Hongu Taisha, Kumano Nachi Taisha, and Kumano Hayatama Taisha. This route is paved with towering trees. The Kumano Hongu Taisha Grand Shrine is one of the holiest places in Japan and a haven for the Shinto faithful.

Wakayama is also the home of the Wakayama Palace and the Seiganto-ji Temple, a tall crimson temple located next to the magnificent Nachi Falls.

❖ What to do there:

a) Relax and take a bath in a hot spring called Kawayu Onsen.

b) Try out traditional long log rafting at Kitayamamura.

c) Visit the old town of Yuasa – the birthplace of the traditional Japanese soy sauce. It is also the home of Kadocho, the oldest soy sauce factory in Japan.

d) You could also visit several temples in the area, such as the Kokawa-dera Temple, Awashima-Jinja Shrine and Asuka-Jinja Shrine.

e) Koyasan Okunoin is a hauntingly beautiful cemetery that records all the key moments of Japanese history. Be sure to get the audio guide in English downtown. It is even better if you join the tour that is run by the monks of the temple.

Nachi Falls

This is the tallest waterfall in Japan. It's 133-meter tall and it stands next to the elegant Seiganto-ji. The spectacular waterfalls gushing through the rock cliffs are truly a sight to behold.

❖ How to get there:

The easiest way is to take a bus at the Kii-Katsura (30mins/600yen) or Nachi Station (20mins/470yen). It is recommended to get off at Daimonzaka and walk there. The walk takes about thirty minutes and you can enjoy the view along the way.

❖ Opening hours:

Shrine office: 6am - 4:30pm

Homotsuden Treasure Hall: 8:30am - 4:30pm / 9am - 4:30pm

(Nov - Mar)

Waterfall viewpoint: 7am - 5pm

❖ Entrance fee:

Shrine grounds: Free

Homotsuden Treasure Hall: Adult - 300 yen, 6-15 years old - 200 yen

Waterfall viewpoint: Adult - 300-yen, Child - 200 yen

❖ Things that you should know before you go there:

a) If you wish to see Nachi Taisha, you need to climb an additional 200-steps to reach the shrine.

b) Public buses run from Nachi every 30 minutes or so. The last one leaves the temple area at around 5:40p.m. so keep an eye on your watch if this is to be your ride home.

c) You could pay an extra 500 yen for a closer look at the waterfall, but you could still very well enjoy the view from the bottom.

d) If you happen to be there on July 14, don't miss the Nachi Fire Festival during which you can see the participants carry large flaming torches to perform an ancient Shinto ritual.

❖ Website and contact:

http://www.kumanonachitaisha.or.jp/

(+81)0735-55-0321

Chapter 3 - Tokyo: Where the Old Meets New

Tokyo is one of the most progressive cities in the world. It's a superpower and just as busy as its Western counterparts.

What's fascinating about Tokyo is that it balances the old and the new. The city is filled with skyscrapers and bright city lights, but it's also filled with relaxing parks and ancient temples. It's also a cultural paradise. The whole city is like a huge theme park.

The Tokyo metro and rail system are one of the best in the world. Riding a Tokyo train is a unique experience. The Japanese fashion is odd but definitely interesting. It's common to see women with pink hair and knee-high socks. You could even find a bunch of young women wearing traditional kimonos while eating french fries at the park.

Tokyo is home to many delicious and special cuisines. It's also a shopping paradise. It's definitely a top destination for foodies, fashion enthusiasts, culture geeks, and technophiles.

You can visit Tokyo anytime. But, if you want to see the famous Sakura or cherry blossoms, you should visit during springtime. The "hanami" or the first bloom of cherry blossoms usually happens during the fourth week of March until the first week of April, which is around 28 March-7 April. But, just to be sure, it's best to check the sakura forecast before you plan your trip because it changes every year.

Neighborhoods
❖ Shibuya
❖ Harajuku
❖ Ginza
❖ Asakusa
❖ Shinjuku
❖ Akihabara
❖ Ueno

Shopping in Tokyo

Tokyo street fashion is unique and far from the traditional kimonos and yukata. Nowadays, Japanese women are wearing short skirts, knee-high socks, sneakers, wedges, shorts, and even haute couture.

The land of the rising sun is the home of one of the most popular clothing brands – Uniqlo. Japan is a shopper's paradise.

Shopping neighborhoods around Japan:

Ginza

Ginza is a posh district in Tokyo and every fashionista's paradise. Its streets are paved with nightclubs, fancy cafes, shops, and departmental stores. You could even find a twelve-story Uniqlo store in the area. Feel the oozing luxury and wealth of the area, while walking along the Ginza Yon-home intersection. Kind of like the Asian equivalent of NYC's busy shopping districts.

You could find all the good things money can buy in Ginza - Shiseido makeup, Louis Vuitton, Mikimoto jewelry, Hermes bags, and Bvlgari jewelry. During weekends, the street will be closed due to vehicular traffic during the day, thus making it a 'pedestrian paradise'. You can just stop and enjoy the scenery or take a few photos without worrying about cars.

❖ Interesting things to do here:

1. The best introduction to Ginza is the Ginza Yon-chome intersection. Find the Ginza Wako Department Store building and its famous clock tower, which is the area's iconic landmark.

2. Shop till you drop! If you want to spend some major yen and if you are a foreigner, bring your passport as you will get tax-free shopping at most of the stores.

3. Ginza's recently opened Kit Kat Chocolatory offers you a selection of Kit Kats with crazy different flavors. From sweet potato to sake-flavored Kit Kats, you can satisfy all your sweet cravings here!

4. If you have time, explore the smaller streets of Ginza as they are filled with smaller shops, restaurants, and cafes that you will never forget.

Harajuku

Harajuku is at the center of Japan's most radical teenage cultures. The district is home to more than one hundred boutiques. One of the streets that you should never miss is the Takeshita Street. You can find plenty of trendy shops, clothes stores, restaurants, and crepe stands there. You can get band shirts, 'princess' style, goth style, and even costumes. That's what makes this street so unique and popular. You can buy everything from boots to earmuffs, and band t-shirts to badges in lots of styles that you might not get at your hometown. Keep an eye out for shops that have promotions for as cheap as $1.

❖ Interesting things to do here:

1. Have some fun with Purikara! The sticker photo booths are the best at Shop NOA, the first store in Japan to be dedicated entirely to Purikara, the shortened version of 'print club' in Japanese.

2. Grab your snacks from Calbee Plus. They specialize in serving hot, crispy potato stick snacks called poterico, and you can top it up with ice-cream or chocolate drizzle. Other than that, Harajuku is also well-known for the countless sweet and savory crepes. Be sure to try one!

3. The largest Daiso in Tokyo is found here. The 100-yen shop is great for purchasing unique Japanese knick-knacks and souvenirs, plus it is extremely budget-friendly.

Shibuya Crossing

It looks a lot like New York City's Time Square and it's one of the most famous tourist spots in Japan. Rumored to be the busiest intersection in the world, Shibuya Crossing has hundreds of people crossing at a time, coming from all directions at once. You can sit in Starbucks (which is the cheapest and the best location) and just watch people go about their day.

❖ Interesting things to do here:

1. You can pose next to the statue of the most loved dog in Japan – Hachiko. Hachiko, an Akita dog, came to Shibuya Station every day to welcome his master back from work. He was so loyal that he kept coming back to Shibuya Station even after his master's death. The statue of this faithful dog is located at the entrance of Shibuya station.

2. Visit Shibuya 109, a shopping mall for youngsters.

3. See the city from Hikarie. The view is the best from the 16th-floor sky lobby. There are also cafes and a Lawson convenience store up there, so you can enjoy the view with a drink. The floors are open until 11pm.

4. Have a delightful feast at Dominique Ansel Bakery! It offers mouth-watering cakes and pastries, and its signature DKA (Dominique's Kouign Amann) - similar to a caramelized croissant - is a must-try. Although there are sister shops in London and New York, some of the pastries can only be found in Japan, so don't miss out on them.

Shinjuku

Slightly classier and less crowded than nearby Shibuya, there are plenty of things to do here. During the day, Shinjuku's massive department stores, from Shinjuku Station eastwards, are a culture all by themselves. Basement floors are a grocery/delicatessen/confectionery cornucopia - full of free munchies, and world-class service at Isetan.

❖ Interesting things to do here:

1. Visit the Tokyo Metropolitan Government Building Observatory. Located in west Shinjuku, this popular, free observatory is open from 9:30am to 11:00pm. There are two towers, and since their closing days don't overlap, one of the decks will always be open.

2. Have a picnic at Shinjuku Gyoen National Garden. It is amazing at the heart of a huge and bustling city. The entry fee is 200 yen and it's a short walk from Takashimaya (Shinjuku gate). The garden is divided into four smaller areas - traditional Japanese garden, English garden, French garden and the greenhouse. There are different exhibitions according to different seasons. It is open from Tuesdays to Sundays, from 9:00a.m. to 4:30p.m.

3. Shinjuku area owns most of the Ramen shops in Tokyo and is often called the most competitive Ramen district. So, if you are a Ramen lover, simply visiting Shinjuku would be the best option.

4. Exiting the east exit of Shinjuku Station, continue in the direction parallel to Yasukuni Dori, and take the cross that is next to Don Quixote. Look up and spot the head of Godzilla peering over the city!

Tokyo Tower

Tokyo Tower is an observation and communication tower in Minato. It's also known as the Eiffel Tower of Tokyo. This red and white structure is a famous Japanese landmark. Like its European counterpart, Tokyo Tower shines brightly at night.

The tower's antenna is used by many networks for broadcasting. You could also find a lot of attractions and restaurants in FootTown- the four-story building located under the tower. For the fans of the anime One Piece, Tokyo One Piece Tower is a must-go as it hosts attractions and restaurants related to the anime.

The main deck that is at a height of 150 meters is open for viewing from 9 am to 11 pm. Last admission is at 10.30pm.

There's a top deck tour every fifteen minutes from 9 am to 10 pm. The tour costs 2800 yen for adults and 1800 yen for children.

❖ Entrance fee:

Adults: 900 yen

Children: 500 yen

❖ How to get there:

You can find Tokyo Tower off the Akabanebashi and Onarimon metro stations.

Places to Visit in Tokyo

The best place to view Tokyo Tower: Sensoji Temple

Sensoji is a red Buddhist temple. It's the oldest temple in Japan as it was built in 645 AD. Like other temples, the complex has a temple hall, an entrance, and a pagoda. The temple has a colorful ceiling and its path is paved with red lanterns and souvenir shops.

Don't forget to stroll down Nakamise-dori.

Nakamise-dori is the shopping street between the Kaminarimon and Hozomon gates of Sensoji Temple. It is 250 meters long. The street, as well as the surrounding streets, is often filled with people wearing traditional kimono, while on the main roads it is possible to go on a rickshaw tour pulled by people wearing old-fashioned clothing.

The narrow street is lined with close to 100 shops that sell everything from snacks to souvenirs and seriously fancy chopsticks. It is a great place to start searching and get some ideas for your souvenirs.

❖ Entrance fee:

Free

❖ Opening hours:

The temple grounds are always open, but the main hall is open from 6 am to 5 pm (Mondays to Sundays from October to March only).

❖ How to get there:

Sensoji Temple is easily accessed via the Asakusa Station. Just follow the signs to the temple and you will find it in no time.

Tokyo Skytree

Tokyo Skytree offers spectacular views of the city. It also hosts a large shopping complex with an aquarium.

❖ How to get there:

Take Tokyo Metro Hanzomon Line or Toei Subway Asakusa Line to go to Oshiage Station.

Top places that you shouldn't miss out on:

Tembo Deck:

Located 350 meters from the ground, you can devour the picturesque scenery of Tokyo from the observation deck. Be sure to check out the four spots called Tokyo Jiku Navi as well. If you are the more adventurous type, don't forget to check out the Glass Floor of Fear, where there's just a piece of glass between you and the air below.

❖ Entrance Fee:

Adult: 2,060 yen

High/Junior high student: 1,540 yen

Child: 930 yen

Infant: 620 yen

❖ Opening hours: 8:00-22:00 (Last admission: 21:00)

Tembo Galleria

Still not high enough for you? Well, check out the Tembo Galleria which stands at a record of 451.2 meters all the way from the ground. Tembo Galleria is ranked as the second tallest observation deck in the world. The best time to visit the observation deck is at night when all the lights are lit up and everything seems so magical.

❖ Entrance Fee:

Adult: 1,030 yen

High/Junior high student: 820 yen

Child: 510 yen

Infant: 310 yen

❖ Opening hours: 8:00-22:00 (Last admission: 21:00)

Sumida Aquarium

Sumida Aquarium is on the 5th floor of the Tokyo Skytree Town. It has natural water scenery, Aqua Gallery and coral reefs. The centerpiece of the aquarium is its 350,000-litre tank, the largest indoor tank in Japan, which is the home to dozens of penguins and several fur seals.

❖ Entrance Fee:

Adult: 2,050 yen

High school student: 1,500 yen

Junior high and elementary student: 1,000 yen

Infant: 600 yen

❖ Opening hours: 9:00-21:00 daily (Last admission: 20:00)

For more information, check out: www.sumida-aquarium.com/en/

Heal yourself at the Konica Minolta planetarium

The planetarium is on the 7th floor of the Tokyo Skytree Town East Yard. It uses state-of-the-art video and sound equipment, which is filled with a sense of realism. The armrest of each seat can also be moved, joining two seats to be used as a couple seat. You can even enjoy different scents during the healing sessions.

❖ Entrance Fee:

Adult: 1,100 yen

Child: 900 yen

Healing planetarium: 1,400 yen

❖ Opening hours:

10:00 to 21:00 daily

Best photo spots to view Tokyo Skytree:

- Asakusa station

- Kototoibashi (bridge)

- Jukken bridge (Stunning Night View)

Toyosu Market and Tsukiji Outer Market

Tsukiji fish market is the largest and busiest fish market in the world. It's a very popular tourist spot. On October 2018, it was moved to Toyosu. It's open all year round and it does not have an entrance fee. The most interesting part is the Tuna Auction; however, there are many other things to see at Toyosu Market. You can enjoy countless street food at Tsukiji outer market, while enjoying the lively atmosphere of the Toyosu Market.

❖ There are also a few restaurants around the area, including:

✓ **Uokame** – This is a luxury restaurant that serves sushi, bouillabaisse, and roasted lobster.

✓ **Tonkatsu Yachiyo** – It's a simple restaurant that specializes in fried food like tonkatsu, chicken katsu, menchi katsu, and kujira katsu. A meal usually costs around $15.

✓ **Torito Bunten** – If you're not a fan of seafood, you should visit Torito Bunten. This restaurant specializes in savory chicken dishes topped with fried egg.

✓ **Ankoya Takahashi** – This restaurant is a bit expensive. But, if you want to really enjoy authentic Japanese food, this is the best place to go. The restaurant serves grilled late spring salmon and steamed red rockfish.

❖ Opening hours: 0400 - 1100 daily except Sunday and alternate Wednesdays.

Meiji Shrine

Meiji Shrine is a Shinto structure dedicated to Emperor Meiji and his wife, Empress Shoken. It was built in 1920 and it's one of the most popular tourist spots in Tokyo. The shrine is made of wood and it's surrounded by trees. It is famous for locals to visit for Hatsumode, first visit to the shrine, during the New Year holidays.

❖ Places to visit in Meiji Shrine:

1. **Treasure Museum of Meiji Jingu,** which is located at the east of the main shrine buildings. The museum is built by the loyal followers of Emperor Meiji as a gift. Treasure Museum Annex is open every day, but the Treasure Hall is only open on Saturdays and Sundays. Photo taking is not allowed inside.

2. **Meiji Shrine Inner Garden.** The garden is 83000 square meters wide and is located between the Meiji Shrine buildings and Yoyogi Park. You will need to pay 500 yen as the entrance fee for the garden. The best time to visit the garden is in the middle of June when all the irises bloom. Don't forget to visit the Kiyomasa's Well as well. This well is well-known for its "power spot", a place for peace and restoration. The emperor and the empress often visited the well.

❖ Entrance Fee:
Meiji Shrine is free to enter. Treasure House and Inner Garden cost 500 yen each.

❖ Opening Hours:
From sunrise to sunset. For New Year's Eve, it specially opens all night for Hatsumode. Treasure House and Inner Garden is open from 9:00a.m. to 4:30p.m.

❖ How to get there:
Take the train to Harajuku Station on the JR Yamanote Line, or Meiji-jingu-mae Station on the Chiyoda and Fukutoshin Subway Lines.

Bonus Tip: If you want to see a traditional Japanese wedding procession, visit this shrine on a Sunday morning.

Tokyo Disneyland (Suggested Time – Two Days)

Disneyland is definitely the happiest place on earth. But, there's something about Tokyo Disneyland that separates it from all the other Disneylands. It's beyond magical. It awakens your inner kid and makes you feel like you're in a storybook. It's simply stunning and extravagant.

❖ The theme park is divided into seven sections:

1. The Fantasyland

2. The Toontown

3. The Tomorrowland

4. The fantastic Critter Country

5. Adventureland

6. The World Bazaar

7. The Westernland.

There are also a variety of rides, such as Space Mountain, Dumbo the Flying Elephant, Alice's Tea Party, and Castle Carousel.

❖ Entrance Fee: The one-day pass costs around 7400 yen for adults, 6400 yen for teens and senior citizens, and 4800 yen for kids.

❖ Opening Hours: From 8 am to 10 pm.

Bonus Tips: You could dance like a Disney princess in Cinderella's Fairy Tale Hall. You also get to see your favorite Disney characters come to life. You can see Alice, Belle, Captain Hook, Cinderella, Esmeralda, Gaston, the Seven Dwarfs, Snow White, and the Mad Hatter in Fantasyland, whereas for Goofy, Mickey Mouse, Minnie Mouse, and Donald Duck, you can find them in Toontown.

Disneyland is magical and marvelous, but it can get very crowded. So, here's a list of things that you should know before going to Tokyo Disneyland:

✓ Get in line at least thirty minutes before the gates open.

✓ Stay at Tokyo Disneyland Hotel for your first day in Tokyo Disneyland. Staying here, or any of the three Disney hotels allow you to enter the park 15 minutes earlier. If it's too expensive for you, you can try the Hilton Tokyo Bay, which is located on the monorail loop.

✓ Bring sunscreen, hats, and a water bottle when you are visiting during summer. Temperate in Tokyo can sometimes reach up to 40 Degree Celsius.

✓ Pack snacks, especially if you're traveling with kids. Restaurants inside cost double.

- ✓ Once you entered the gates, the first things to do is run to Monsters, Inc. Ride & Go Seek. Use the shortcut through World Bazaar into Tomorrowland to get Fast Passes and then race to Fantasyland.

- ✓ Between the Peter Pan' Flight and Pooh ride, go for Peter Pan's Flight first (no longer have Fast Pass). Pooh typically has a short line when the park is almost near to closing.

- ✓ Make sure to check out the must-do attractions such as Haunted Mansion, Space Mountain, Roger Rabbit's Car Toon Spin and Pirates of the Caribbean. Get a Fast Pass for the Space Mountain and Haunted Mansion.

- ✓ Go Car Toon Spin early, as it normally has super long lines and doesn't have Fast Pass.

Tokyo Disney Sea

DisneySea is just a mile away from Disneyland and it's also located in Tokyo Disney Resort. DisneySea is much smaller compared to Disneyland.

Tokyo Disneyland is a bit similar to the original theme park located in Orlando, Florida. However, DisneySea is something that you can only see in Tokyo. It's unique and has a fantastic landscape. You will feel like you're in a lost world. The park mimics the beauty of fancy Mediterranean seascapes. The mermaid lagoon looks exactly like the one in the animated film. The coral castle is colorful and dreamy.

The shows have a running nautical theme, but they're simply magical. You should not miss King Triton's Concert. It's colorful, whimsical, and simply out of this world.

When it comes to the differences between Tokyo Disneyland and DisneySea, it is important to state that DisneySea is more 'adult-friendly' as it not only offers fewer attraction rides for kids but also provides alcoholic drinks.

❖ The theme park has seven areas:

1. The Mediterranean Harbor

2. The American Waterfront

3. The Port Discovery

4. The Lost River Delta

5. The Arabian Coast

6. The Mermaid Lagoon

7. The Mysterious Island.

❖ Things you should know before going to DisneySea:

1. Always Arrive Early – If you're staying at the MiraCosta, be there at least 30 minutes before the park opening. If you're staying at non-Disney hotels, you will need to be there even earlier.
2. Toy Story Mania is the most popular attraction in the whole Disney sea. The crowds there are seriously crazy. Even the Fast Pass have long lines. So, you should totally skip this. Trust me, it's not worth the time. It's actually more or less the same as the US versions.
3. Go for the Tower of Tower instead of Toy Story Mania. This one is very different from those found in the US parks. Go for the Fast Passes for this ride. My recommendation is to send one person here to buy the fast passes, while the rest of you head towards the Journey to the Center of the Earth.
4. Try their popcorn at least once. The popcorns there are no ordinary popcorns. They are very well-known all throughout the world among Disney fans. They offer a variety of flavors as well.

❖ Entrance Fee:

One day pass costs around 7400 yen for adults (18 – 59), 6400 yen for teens and senior citizens, and 4800 yen for kids (11 and below).

❖ Opening Hours:

From 8:30 am to 10:00 am from Monday to Sunday.

Imperial Palace and East Garden

Imperial Palace is one of the most beautiful palaces in Tokyo. It is the residence of the emperor of Japan. In the 1980s, the value of the castle and its surrounding properties was more than the value of all the real estate properties in California.

The palace is located in Chiyoda, Tokyo. It has white walls and an elegant brown roof. It was completed in 1888. Although it was bombed during the second world war, it was reconstructed afterward. It lies on top of a hill beside the beautiful Nijubashi Bridge. It's about ten minutes from Tokyo station, so it's easily accessible.

The emperor is still currently residing in this palace. So, please be aware that the rules are quite strict around here. No drones are allowed in this area.

English guided tours of the palace grounds are available throughout the year except on Sundays and Mondays. A typical tour will last for 75 minutes. Reservations can be made either through the Imperial Household Agency official website or at the Kikyomon Gate.

Visitors can only visit the castle gardens.

❖ Entrance fee:

Free

❖ Opening hours:

- March 1 to April 14 – 9 am to 430 pm
- April 15 to August 30 – 9 am to 5 pm
- September 1 to October 30 – 9 am to 430 pm
- November 1 to February 29 – 9 am to 4 pm

The palace garden is closed every Friday and Monday. It's also closed during special holidays.

Ghibli Museum

Are you an anime fan? If you are, you should totally head to the Ghibli Museum in Mitaka, Tokyo. The museum showcases the work of Hayao Miyazaki's Studio Ghibli, which is the famous animation company that has produced films like "Spirited Away" and "Ponyo". You will also be able to see models of the characters of the popular animated fantasy film called "My Neighbour Totoro". This whimsical museum will transport you into a fantasy world.

Exhibitions are held on the first floor. There is also a small theater showcasing short Ghibli movies. Visit the second floor for special temporary exhibitions. There is also a play area for kids, a reading room full of books recommended by the museum, and a beautiful roof-top garden that features character sculptures.

❖ Entrance fee:

Adults: 1000 yen

Teens (13 -18): 700 yen

Children (7-12): 400 yen

Toddlers (4-6): 100 yen

Babies and toddlers (below 4 years old): Free of charge

❖ How to get there:

Get off at Mitaka Station on the JR Chuo Line, which will cost 220 yen and 15 minutes from Shinjuku Station. Then, take the museum shuttle bus (210-yen one way, 320-yen roundtrip; children can get half price tickets). You can also walk from Mitaka Station to the museum through Inokashira Park. It takes about 20 minutes to reach there.

❖ Opening Hours:

10:00 to 18:00 from Wednesday to Monday.

Akihabara

Akihabara or Akiba is the hub of many electronic shops. If you're looking for a new gadget, this is the best place to go. It's also Tokyo's manga and anime paradise. You'd see robot statues, anime coffee shops, and cosplayers around the district.

The top five must-see spots in Akihabara:

1. Yodobashi Camera

When it comes to electrical goods, they have everything you can think of. This is an enormous retail outlet, which you can't find in the US. Their staffs are also highly trained and very knowledgeable about their electrical appliances. You can find lots of promotions here as well due to the very competitive neighborhood.

❖ How to get there:

Central entrance. You won't miss it.

❖ Store hours:

9:30 a.m. to 10 p.m. daily

2. Walk along Chuo Dori

This is the main street of Akihabara. Take some time to walk around this street and experience what Akihabara truly offers. You should explore the branch off alleys after that. Some of the shops in the alleys are much cheaper.

3. Mandarake

This is one of Akihabara's biggest shop when it comes to collectibles. They sell all kinds of collectibles ranging from mascots, manga comics to rare anime figures.

Bonus Tip: Start from the eighth floor which is the top and slowly work your way down.

4. AKB48 Cafe/Shop

AKB48 is an extremely popular J-pop group made up of forty-eight girls. They even have branches all throughout Asia. AKB actually stands for Akihabara because everything about them originated here. You can find all sorts of sweets and lots of AKB48 photos in the cafe.

❖ Cafe Hours:
Weekdays: 11a.m.-11p.m.
Weekends and holidays: 10 a.m.-11 p.m.
Shop Hours:
Monday to Thursday: 11a.m.-10p.m.
Friday and Saturday: 11a.m.-10:30p.m.

Sunday and holidays: 10a.m.-10p.m.

❖ How to get there:

On the right of west exit. Under the tracks.

5. Gundam Café

This café sells all sorts of Gundam goods. Even their food is Gundam-themed. Their staff are also all dressed in Gundam uniforms. They will snap a salute when they take your order. They offer take out as well if you are in a rush.

Bonus Tips: Don't forget to try out their special character lattes.

❖ Cafe hours:

Weekdays: 10 a.m. - 11 p.m.
Saturday: 8:30 a.m. - 11 p.m.
Sundays and holidays: 8:30 a.m. - 9:30 p.m.

❖ How to get there:

It is located right beside AKB 48 café.

Sumo at Ryoguku Kokugikan

Sumo is the national sport of Japan, dating back to ancient times, and it is also one of the most unique and interesting cultures in Japan. Only three of six official grand tournaments are held in Tokyo, all at Ryoguku Kokugikan. Watching Sumo wrestlers in action at such a close distance is totally breathtaking. It's not a cheap activity for every traveler, but it's worth the money and one of the most precious experiences you can have in Japan.

Instead of the tournaments, you can also choose to visit the home ground of Sumo wrestlers and have a glimpse of the real lives of these wrestlers. A number of Sumo stables, which are the training rooms for the Sumo wrestlers are located in Tokyo, especially in the Ryogoku area.

Some of the Sumo stables are open to the public and visitors can see the morning training sessions up close. The training session is also known as Keiko. You can not only observe the wrestlers' dynamic and powerful actions, but also learn the Japanese tradition and discipline, which you may not see often in this era.

❖ Here are some stables where you can watch Keiko:

- Musashigawa Beya in Uguisudani

- Kasugano Beya near Ryoguku Station

- Takasago Beya near Asakusa Station

You can also watch the training session at Arashio Sumo Stable, but you can only stand outside the building and watch it through a large window. This is ideal if you only want to watch for a brief moment and take a few pictures.

❖ Time: The time for Keiko varies from stable to stable, but it usually starts at around 6am, or 7am and lasts for around 3 hours. Practice is not normally held on a weekend, and after the tournament, the wrestlers usually take a break for a week.

Tokyo National Museum

If you plan to visit only one museum in Tokyo, Tokyo National Museum should be the one. Strolling through the halls of its buildings, you can admire the world's largest collection of Japanese art, including samurai armor and swords, colorful woodblock prints, delicate pottery, kimonos, calligraphy, paintings, and many more.

If you only have a couple of hours to spare, you should focus on the Honkan (Japanese Gallery) and the enchanting Gallery of Hotyu-ji Treasures. With more time, you can explore the three-story Toyokan (Gallery of Asian Art).

The museum features English translations for most of its exhibits, but the temporary exhibitions hosts might lack the English signage. The Museum Garden behind Honkan will be open to the public during autumn.

❖ Entrance fee:

Adults: 620 yen

University students: 410 yen

Other visitors (under 18 and over 70): Free

*Free admission to regular exhibitions on International Museum Day (18 May for 2019) and Respect for the Aged Day (16 September for 2019)

❖ Opening hours:

09:30 - 17:00 (Last admission: 16:30) Tuesday to Sunday.

*Open until 21:00 on Fridays and Saturdays.

❖ How to get there:

A 10-minute walk from Ueno, or Uguisudani Station.

Jimbocho

If you are a book lover, head to the second largest second-hand book market in the world, Jimbocho. It houses over 170 bookshops, publishing houses and literary societies. There are also non-Japanese titles available as well.

Kitazawa Bookstore is one of the shops that you should pay a visit to. You can enjoy a wide selection of books including those from the English Middle Ages with comfy seats and gigantic soft toys!

❖ How to get there:

Take the train to Jimbocho Station and exit by Exit A1, then walk to the right.

What to Eat in Tokyo

Tokyo is the land of the best Japanese dishes – sushi, ramen, tempura, sashimi, soba, udon, and soba.

Many tourists head to the fisherman restaurants to get their hands on some authentic sushi. But, if you want to save money and avoid the flock of tourists, you can go to the Ougashi Nihon-chi Standing Sushi Bar in downtown Shibuya. You can get a platter of squid, red tuna, salmon, and scallop nigiris for less than $8.

The standing sushi bar in Minato is just as good as the one in Shibuya. The Uohgashi Nihonichi Shimbashi Hibiyaguchi is located in Shimbashi, Minato. This restaurant offers a wide variety of sushi, including unagi (eel), aka ebi (big, sweet shrimp), uni (sea urchin), aburi salmon, and ootoro (fatty tuna belly).

❖ The best restaurants in the city:

✓ **Ise Sueyoshi (Minato)** – This restaurant is good for fine dining. It has exemplary customer service and great food. It is known for their delicious tempura, matcha tea, sake, and teppanyaki. The average cost of each meal is 19500 yen or $90. It opens during lunchtime and closes at 11 pm.

✓ **Han No Daidokoro (Shibuya)** – This restaurant is best for barbecue and other meat dishes. It's open during lunchtime and closes at 11 pm. Lunch costs around 1000 yen and dinner costs around 5000 yen. This mid-priced restaurant gives you the best value for your money.

✓ **Ippudo Roppongi (Minato)** – This restaurant is best for budget travelers. They serve delicious and cheap ramens and other traditional Japanese dishes. Many people believe that this restaurant serves the best ramen in Tokyo. Its price range is at 750 to 1500 yen.

Where to Stay in Tokyo

It's no secret that accommodations in Tokyo are a bit expensive. However, there are still plenty of beautiful and affordable hotels around the city. Here is a list of hotels that I personally recommend:

✓ Sakura Hotel and Hostel Jimbucho, from $28 per night

✓ Tokyo Green Hotel (Korakuen), from $68 per night

✓ Hotel Asia Center of Japan, from $153 per night

✓ Khaosan World Asakusa Ryokan and Hostel, from $31 per night

✓ Anne Hostel Asakusabashi, from $30 per night

Capsule Hotel

If you are not on a tight budget, try checking out capsule hotels like Capsule and Sauna Century Shibuya, and Sauna Ikebukuro Plaza.

Capsule and Sauna Century Shibuya (2-star):

Capsule and Sauna Century is a male-only accommodation. They offer facilities such as large hot tubs, coin launderette, massage chairs, free internet PCs, free Wi-Fi and saunas. You can expect a free TV, alarm clock, radio, and yukata robe as well. Meals are not provided, but there are plenty of restaurants nearby if you ever get hungry.

It is located in Shibuya, a 5-minute walk away from Shibuya Station. Some of the popular destinations nearby are Tokyo Shrine, Tokyo Tower, Shinjuku and Harajuku (7-minute train ride).

Prices are from 3400 yen per night.

Capsule and Sauna Ikebukuro Plaza (2-star):

Capsule and Sauna Ikebukuro Plaza is a women-only accommodation. They offer facilities such as a large communal bath, stylish saunas, free Wi-Fi, restaurant, laundry, TV, radio alarm clock, and trouser press.

It is located near the West Exit of Ikebukuro Station. You can walk there in 5 minutes.

Airbnb

When it comes to Tokyo Airbnb, avoid the areas in big cities. Staying in big cities will be expensive. Instead, look out for places that are near to a train, or bus station. You really don't want to walk an extra 5Km after a long day trip. Check out areas such as Kita.

Chapter 4 - Kyoto: Home of More Than A Thousand Temples

Kyoto used to be the capital of the imperial Japan until 1868. It's one of the most beautiful cities in the land of the rising sun. It's the home to one thousand Buddhist temples, around four hundred colorful shrines, Zen gardens, and even a few Samurai castles.

Kyoto is also the birthplace of the intriguing geisha culture. Contrary to common Western belief, *geishas* are not prostitute. They are entertainers who have mastered the art of music and dance. They're graceful, gentle, and beautiful. However, some *geisha* may choose to engage in a sexual relationship with a customer that she's fond of. You could literally see mysterious *geisha* and *maiko* (apprentices) walking freely in the city, especially around Gion.

But Kyoto is more than just the land of the Geishas. It is also the home of architectural and cultural gems. It is a city unlike any other that is sure to captivate your heart and soul.

Places to Visit in Kyoto

Kiyomizu-dera Temple

Kiyomizu-dera means Pure Water Temple. Built in 780, it was purely made of wood. It is especially known for its wooden stage outside its main hall as it was made without nails. The stage houses the temple's most significant object of worship, Kannon, which is a statue with eleven faces and a thousand arms.

There are approximately 1500 cherry blossom trees in the area of the temple. It looks exceptionally beautiful during spring and autumn, with scenery that allows you to revel in a sea of colors. The temple gives you a wide, good view of the Kyoto cityscape as well.

❖ What else you can see around the temple:

1. 3-storey tall Koyasu Pagoda, which is believed to bring safe and easy childbirth

2. Okunion Hall, along with more halls just beside it, dedicated to Shaka Buddha and Amida Buddha

3. Stone statues of Jizo, the protector of children and travelers

4. The "Mother's Womb", a pitch-black basement, with a little bit of add-on admission fee

5. Jishu Shrine, dedicated for love or matchmaking

6. Belfry, a humungous 2.3-ton bell

7. Spring Illumination (Hanami) from mid-March to mid-April: 6pm – 9pm

8. Fall Illumination, mid-November to early-December: 6pm - 9pm

❖ Other events include:

1. April: Miyako Odori (traditional annual spring dance)

2. 15th of May: Aoi Matsuri (a parade from Imperial Palace to Kamo Shrines)

3. July: Gion Matsuri, Yoiyama (Kyoto's Magical Night), Yamaboko Junko (float procession)

4. October: Jidai Matsuri (Festival of Ages)

❖ Opening hours:

6am – 6pm all year round; the temple is open until 9pm during the illumination events.

❖ Entrance fee:

400 yen

*Entrance fee may differ according to the season.

❖ How to get there:

1. From Kyoto Station, bus number 100 or 206 (10-20 minutes, 230 yen), and get off at either Goio-zaka or Kiyomizu-michi bus stop, then take a 10-minute walk to the temple.

2. From Kiyomizu-Gojo Station, about 20 minutes of walking along the Keihan Railway Line.

Bonus Tip: The main temple is under renovation as of December 2018 and it will likely take a year or so. The area is still lively with many restaurants and souvenir shops, but you may avoid the 600-yen entry fee.

Nishiki Market

The Nishiki Market is a long and narrow shopping street in Kyoto. It's often called "Kyoto's kitchen" because the city's top chefs and home cooks go there for the best local ingredients. You can find a number of fresh tofu, wagashi or Japanese desserts, sashimi, shellfish, tea, and fish here. You could also find pickled vegetables called Nukazuke. One of the best things about the Nishiki market is that you can haggle and get the best possible price.

❖ Opening hours:

9:30 am to 6 pm daily, but many shops are closed on Wednesdays.

❖ How to get there:

The Nishiki Market street runs along the Shijo Avenue. It's a five-minute walk from Shijo Station on the Karasuma Subway Line.

❖ Things you could do there:

1. Visit **Aritsugu**, the oldest knife crafting shop in Japan. You will be surprised at how different knives are made for different ingredients.

2. Try the *tsukemono* (pickled vegetables) at **Uchida Tsukemono**. It can be easily identified by its large wooden barrels of pickled goods.

3. Order deep fried *hamo* (pike conger) and boiled hamo teriyaki at **Uoriki**. Be ready to order when you are at the front of the line, or the owner might just skip you!

4. Have a blast at **Konno Monja** if you are a tofu-lover. They sell a variety of items including tofu ice-cream and crispy tofu donuts.

5. Enjoy the fish sticks at **Sakana Kushi**. Each stick costs only 200 yen.

6. If you have a sweet tooth, don't miss out the chocolate *korokke* (deep-fried bread filled with chocolate) there!

Bonus Tip: Bear in mind that walking while eating is frowned upon in this market, so if you buy some snacks it's best to sit down and eat it or take it home.

Fushimi-Inari-Taisha Shrine

The Fushimi Inari Shrine is one of the most renowned sites in Kyoto, and also one of the most prominent Shinto shrines in Southern Kyoto. It is well-known for its near five thousand bright red Torii gates, lined up to form a path to the sacred Mount Inari, which stands around 230-metre tall. The shrine was built in 711, one of the oldest structures in Japan, dedicated to Inari, the Shinto god of rice and sake.

There are also dozens of fox statues, representing the messengers of the god of grain food. While this shrine is a sacred place for worship, most foreign visitors come here to tour the mountain trails and take stunning photographs.

At the entrance stands the Romon Gate, which was donated by Toyotomi Hideyoshi in 1589. The far side of the main hall is where visitors usually pay respect to the gods by making offerings. And near that is the entrance to the Torii gate trails. All of these gates are sponsored by individuals or companies, with their names and the date of donation engraved on each gate. The smaller gates cost around 400,000 yen and for the bigger ones, over 1 million yen.

The journey on foot to the summit and back usually takes around 2-3 hours, but visitors are free to stroll around freely without any time limit. Along the way, there are numerous shrines with smaller Torii gates donated by visitors. There are also some restaurants with local dishes such as sushi, udon and aburaage (fried tofu). Around halfway through the hike (about half an hour hike), there's the Yotsutsuji Intersection, where visitors can have a pleasant view of Kyoto.

❖ Notable events:

1. 1st of January: Saitan-sai (New Year's Prayers)

2. 12th of April: Minakuchi Hashu-sai (Rice seedlings are planted into nursery beds and prayers are offered for protection of Inari, to produce lush harvest)

3. 10th of June: Rice seedlings previously planted are transferred into shrine paddies, prayers are also offered

4. 25th of October: Harvested rice is offered up for Shinjo-sai (November 23)

5. 31st of December: Oharae-shiki (A purification ceremony to efface sins committed, and to start a new year in the state of clarity)

❖ Entrance fee:

Free

❖ Opening hours:

Open 24/7 throughout the year

❖ How to get there:

The Fushimi Inari Shrine is just five minutes away from Kyoto Station via the JR Nara Line, for about 140 yen. Apart from that, it can also be reached by taking a short walk along the Keihan Mainline from Fushimi Inari Station.

Bonus Tip: The best time to visit the shrine is early in the morning, or late in the evening. It usually gets really crowded by 10am.

Arashiyama Bamboo Grove

Bamboos are tall, slender, and incredibly strong trees. The pathway of Arashiyama Bamboo Grove is paved with bamboo trees. It is no doubt one of the most photographed attractions in Arashiyama, but no picture can capture the experience of standing in the midst of these sky-scraping bamboo trees. This place is incredibly relaxing and peaceful as well.

❖ Things that you should know before you go there:

1. Be sure to visit the **Togetsukyo Bridge**, where you can see the whole view of Arayashima forest, mountain and river.

2. One of the best ways to enjoy Arashiyama is by cycling. Bicycles are available near the train station for around 1000yen.

3. There are also lots of temples around and you can cycle all the way to them such as to Tenryuji Temple, Daikakuji Temple, Jojakkoji Temple, Nisonin Temple, and so on.

❖ Entrance fee:

Free

❖ Opening hours:

Open every day from 9 am to 5 pm

❖ How to get there:

A 10-min walk from Saga Arashiyama Station, JR Sagano line.

Alternatively, a 15-min walk from Arashiyama Station, Henkyu railway.

Bonus Tip: Come as early as 6am in the morning when the crowds haven't arrived to capture the full experience of Arashiyama Bamboo Grove.

Recommendation: The temples around such as Tenryuji Temple and Daikakuji Temple are very beautiful, especially during the cherry blossom period and autumn. However, you may want to skip the temples around here during winter. There is nothing much to see except for the temple itself.

Kinkaku-ji Temple

The Kinkakuji, or the Golden Pavilion is a Zen temple. It was once the retirement home of a military dictator named Ashikaga Yoshimitsu. It was built in 1393. The huge house sits beside a vast pond and it's surrounded by lilies and lush green trees. What makes this temple stand out is that its second and third floors are literally covered with gold. You should not miss this one when you're in Japan. It's not every day that you get to see a house made of gold.

❖ Entrance fee:

Adults - 400 yen, children - 300 yen

❖ Opening hours:

Open every day from 9 am to 5pm

❖ How to get there:

Take a direct Kyoto City Bus number 101 or 205 from Kyoto Station (40 minutes and for 230 yen)

For a faster and more reliable route, you can also take the Karasuma Subway Line to Kitaoji Station (15 minutes, 260 yen), where Kyoto City Buses number 101, 102, 204 and 205 will take you to Kinkakuji-michi bus stop (10 minutes).

Bonus Tip: If possible, go there on a Monday morning to beat the crowds.

Nijo Castle

Nijo Castle is one of the most imposing and unique UNESCO world heritage structures in Kyoto. It was the residence of the first *shogun* (military commander) of the Edo Period named Tokugawa Lesayu. The intentionally squeaky floors were used as security for the *shogun*. You could also find a garden called Ninomaru Teien in the area.

❖ Opening hours:

Open from 8:45 am to 5 pm. It is closed every Tuesday of January, July, August, and December. It's also closed from December 26th to January 4th.

❖ Entrance fee:

600 yen

❖ How to get there:

Take the Karasuma Subway Line to Karasuma-Oike Station from Kyoto Station. Then, transfer to the Tozai Line and get off at Nijojo-mae Station (15 minutes and costs 260 yen). The entrance of Nijo Castle is a short walk from Nijojo-mae Station. You can also reach the castle by bus 9, 50 or 101 for a cheaper fare (15 minutes, 230-yen one way).

Bonus Tip: You can skip Nijo Castle if you are going to Osaka Castle as they are about the same. Osaka Castle is much bigger and grander compared to Nijo Castle. There will be lots of walking (at least 5km in the inner castle itself), so be prepared and stay hydrated.

Ginkaku-ji (The Silver Pavillion)

Here's what's weird about the Ginkaku-ji – it does not actually contain silver. It was built as a retirement home of the *shogun* (military dictator). The founder, whose grandfather built the Golden Pavillion, intended to cover the main structure in silver and therefore named it accordingly, but the plan was never carried out.

It's a beautiful temple with interesting landscapes. This lavish house has a garden and a pond surrounded by comforting trees. The garden looks vibrant and oozes with colors and texture during the autumn season.

Visitors can also access Ginkakuji's moss garden and hill, which features ponds, small waterfalls, bridges and lots of moss. From the hill behind, you can witness the grand view of the entire temple.

Don't forget to check out the Philosopher's path as well after exiting. You will reach Eikan-do temple if you walk along the path.

❖ Opening hours:

8:30 am to 5 pm (March to November) and 9am to 4:30pm (December to February).

❖ Entrance fee:

Adults - 500 yen, Children - 300 yen

❖ How to get there:

From Kyoto Station, take a direct bus no. 5, 17 or 100 (35-40 minutes and for 230 yen).

Bonus Tip: You can skip this temple if you plan to visit the Kinkaku-ji temple. They are more or less the same. However, this smaller pavilion, set in a large and beautiful garden, is less crowded and thus more relaxing to walk around.

Amanoshashidate

This is one of Kyoto's best-kept secrets. It's a long sandbar that connects the two sides of Mizayu bay. It's made of pure white sand and lined with evergreen trees. You could get a good view of the sandbar by riding a cable car.

If you have spare time, it would be a good idea to walk on the sand bar, which takes about 45 minutes one-way.

❖ How to get there:

The sandbar is located two hours away from Osaka Station and Kyoto Station. You can just take a train from downtown Kyoto Station. Once you have reached the Amanoshasidate Station, you just have to walk to the cable car that's going to take you to the sandbar. Do take note that you still need to pay approximately 4500 yen for the trip even if you have a JP pass.

Alternatively, you can take a bus over from Kyoto, which is cheaper and takes more or less the same duration of time. You can reserve return tickets to go there at the JR counter.

❖   Things that you should know before you go there:

1. If possible, take Tango Akamatsu train (extra 500 yen) from Fukuchiyama as the train takes the path within rarely visited yet beautiful places.

2. There are bicycles for rent if you don't want to walk.

3. Make sure that you reach there early in the morning. Most of the shops are closed by 4:30p.m.

4. You can also get a 12-minute boat cruise around the bay for 530 yen each way.

❖   Entrance fee:

Free, but you will have to pay 800 yen for the chairlift ride.

Bonus Tip: If you want to visit as many places as you can in Kyoto within a short time, you should consider skipping here as the train ride is quite time-consuming.

If you choose to come here, do allocate an entire day to enjoy the whole experience.

Ryoan-ji

The reason that the rock garden was built is still a mystery. It is widely believed that it is meant to be a riddle designed by a Zen master for his students.

Once you enter the temple, you can see rocks with various shapes in the sand from the balcony of the *Hojo* (the head priest's former residence). It is said that you would obtain enlightenment if you can gain a view of all the fifteen rocks at the same time. Meanwhile, it is believed that if you focus your mind on only one rock, you can improve your concentration and bring focus to achieve your hopes and purpose in life.

How much the rock garden will resonate is a matter of personal aesthetics and relative circumstances. However, you should not miss the temple grounds that include the Pilgrim's Path and Tsukubai, which is a unique stone-wash basin. It would be a satisfying experience to slow down and do a full circle around the lake there.

❖ Opening hours:

8:00 am to 5 pm (March to November) and 8:30 am to 4:30pm (December to February).

❖ Entrance fee:

Adults - 500 yen, Children - 300 yen

❖ How to get there:

1. From the Kyoto Station, take bus number 50 and get off at Ritsumeikan Daigaku-mae bus stop (30 minutes, 230 yen) and walk for around 7 minutes. You can use your JR pass too if you have bought one.

2. From Ninnaji or the Golden Pavillion, you can walk there in 20 minutes, or take a 5-minute bus ride.

Bonus Tips: Like a lot of other popular tourist places, you should be there early in the morning, or just before the closing time. The crowds can be pretty thick by mid-day, especially the rock garden. Also, the entrance fee is only for the rock garden. You can enjoy the rest of the gorgeous temple grounds within the premises for free.

Gion

Gion is popular as the spot to see *geisha* (or, properly speaking, *geiko* and *maiko* - fully fledged and trainee *geisha* respectively). If you aim to find one, you should go there in the evening, which is the time for the *geisha* to go to work.

Walk down the main street Hanami-koji, and visit one of Kyoto's most beautiful streets, Shimbashi/Shirakawa Minami-dori. The well-preserved shrines and temples along with the arts and crafts will give you a little sneak peek into Japan's past. Nonetheless, the streets are full of shops and restaurants, bustling with visitors.

To really appreciate the beauty of *geisha* culture, it is recommended to watch one of the dances performed by the *geisha* each year. You can ask at the Kyoto Tourist Information Center, or at your lodgings for help with ticket purchase.

❖ How to get there:

Take bus number 100 or 26 (20minutes, 230 yen) at Kyoto Station and get off at Gion bus stop. Alternatively, the closest train stations are Gion Shijo Station and Kawaramachi Station.

Kyoto Food Guide

Matcha Heaven

Kyoto has the best matcha desserts in the entire world. Matcha parfait, shaved ice, soft-serve, ice-cream... you should try them all in Kyoto!

#1 Gion Kinana

Visit this popular ice cream shop located on the famous Gion street. Do try out the signature matcha parfait and soy bean ice-cream. The famed 'dekitate' ice-cream i.e. ice-cream freshly made and never frozen is a must-try too!

Opening hours: 11am - 7pm daily

Address: 570-119 Gioncho Minamigawa, Kyoto

#2 Kagizen Yoshifusa

You can also visit this traditional Japanese dessert shop located in Higashiyama-Ku. Enjoy the traditional desserts with a cup of matcha. First-timers should try Kuzukiri, which is a bowl of translucent noodles made of arrowroot with a sweet brown syrup.

Opening hours: 9:30am - 6pm (Tue - Sun)

Address: 264 Gionmachi Kitagawa, Higashiyama-ku

Bonus Tip: Take note that everyone has to place an order there, that is, you cannot simply order one dessert and share.

#3 Kyo Hayashiya

If your sole love in life is matcha, you should totally go to this place. There are lots of matcha or koucha (English tea) menus. The matcha parfait and the matcha cheesecake set are highly recommended.

Opening hours: 11:30am - 7pm (Mon - Tue), 11:30am - 8pm (Wed), 11:30am - 9:30pm (Thurs - Sun)

Address: 105 Nakajimacho, Takasa Building. 6F, Nakagyo

The Best, Affordable Sushi in Kyoto:

#1 Sushisei

They offer the best price when it comes to sushi. They are also very friendly and welcoming to foreigners.

Opening hours: 11:30am to 3pm, 5pm - 10pm daily

Address: B1 Daimaru department store, Shijo-Takakura Parking Building, 581 Obiya-cho, Takakura-dori Nishikikoji sagaru, Nakagyo-ku

A 4-minute walk from Shijo Station or Karasuma Station

#2 Den Shichi

Classic style sushi-bar with super fresh sushi.

Opening hours: 11:30am to 2pm, 5pm - 10:30pm (Tue - Sun)

Address: 4-1 Tatsumi-cho, Saiin, Ukyo-ku

A 4-minute walk from Saiin Station

#3 Ganko Sushi.

Friendly and helpful staff together with reasonably priced sushi make them one of the best.

Opening hours: 11am -11pm daily

Address: 101 Nakajima-cho, Sanjo-dori, Kawaramachi Higashi iru, Nakagyo-ku

A 3-minute walk from Sanjo Station

The Best Ramen in Kyoto:

#1 Ippudo.

The best ramen joint in the whole of Japan. Gyoza is extremely delicious too!

Opening hours: 11am - 2am (Sun), 11am - 3am (Mon - Sat)

Address: 653-1 Bantoya-cho, Higashinotoin, Nishikikoji higashi iru, Nakagyo-ku

A 2-minute walk from Shijo Station

#2 Karako.

They serve the best roasted sliced pork ramen. *Karaage* (fried chicken) here is famous too.

Opening hours: 11:30am to 2pm, 6pm - 12am (Wed - Mon)

Address: 12-3 Tokusei-cho, Okazaki, Sakyo-ku

A 9-minute walk from Jingu Marutamachi Station

#3 Ramen Muraji.

They serve the best chicken broth ramen. They are also famous for their fast and polite service.

Opening hours: 11:30am - 3pm, 5pm - 10pm (Mon - Fri), 11:30am - 10pm (Sat), 11:30am - 8pm (Sun)

Address: 373-3 Kiyomotocho, Higashiyama-ku, Kyoto

A 2-minute walk from Gion-Shijo

The Best Cafes in Kyoto:

#1 Café Bibliotic HELLO!

A machiya style, uber-hip café. Do note that they do not accept credit cards.

Opening hours: 11:30am - 12am daily

Address: 650 Seimei-cho, Yanaginobanba-higashi-iru, Nijo-dori, Nakagyo-ku

A 7-minute walk from Karasuma Oike Station Exit 1

#2 Inoda Coffee

The best old and local coffee shop. Try out their breakfast set, which is a great value for money!

Opening hours: 8am - 8pm (Sun - Thurs), 8am - 9pm (Fri & Sat)

Address: 140 Doyu-cho, Sanjo-sagaru, Sakaimachi-dori, Nakagyo-ku

A 4-minute walk from Karasuma Oike Station Exit 5

#3 %Arabica.

A modern and stylish cafe with great coffee. There is always a queue here, so try to come here early.

Opening hours: 8am - 6pm daily

Address: 87-5 Hoshino-cho, Higashiyama-ku

Take bus 206 from Kyoto Station to Higashiyama Yasui Bus Stop. The cafe is located at a 5-minute walk away from the bus stop.

Kyoto Accommodation Guide

Again, it is best to stay near the stations so that you can commute easily.

#1 Tawaraya

If money is not an issue to you, Tawaraya is one of the finest places to stay. It's a very warm and intimate *ryokan*, with the best of everything. It's centrally located and you can easily walk to the subway stations and various good restaurants.

Address: 278 Nakahakusancho, Fuyacho, Oike-sagaru, Nakagyo-ku

Take Tozai line to Kyoto-Shiyakusho station

#2 Capsule Ryokan Kyoto

The ryokan-style capsules here are special as well as comfortable. The private rooms have all the amenities that you may need, including bathrooms.

Address: 204 Tsuchihashi-cho, Shimogyo-ku

A 7-minute walk from Kyoto Station. If you don't want to walk, take bus number 206 and stop at Higashiyama-Dori Street.

#3 Lowest East 9

It is a quiet hostel with spacious capsule-style dorms. It is conveniently located right next to Kujo Station.

Address: 32 Higashikujo, Minamikarasuma, Minami-ku

A 1-minute walk from Kujo subway station. Alternatively, a 10-minute walk from Kyoto Station.

Chapter 5 -: Bright Osaka Lights and Magic

Osaka is a thriving, enchanting city that could fill anyone with wonder, magic and excitement. If Tokyo is what we call a shining jewel, Osaka would be old gold, still shiny, but with just the right hint of nicks and cuts in the dulled reflection. The one thing that sets apart Osaka from all other cities in Japan is its resilience. Centuries ago, the city was practically demolished during the Second World War, but through hard work, blood, sweat and tears, it was rebuilt again at a rapid pace. The Osaka as we know today exists because of its tragic history, but like a phoenix, it rose from the ashes, justifying a story of resiliency. Today, Osaka has become the second biggest city in Japan.

I have done tours in Osaka for years and the city truly never gets old. Here's a list of the tourist spots in Osaka:

Top Tourist Spots in Osaka

Osaka Castle

This magnificent piece of architecture is an Eastern castle, which was built by a Japanese politician and warrior named Toyotomi Hideyoshi. It was built in 1583 and it was once the biggest castle in Japan. It's located right beside the Nishinomaru garden, which contains over five hundred cherry trees! The castle was sieged and attacked when Toyotomi died, but the castle's ferocious concrete walls protected it from major damages. It has even survived air raids during the war.

❖ How to get there:
Take the subway to Tanimachi 4-chrome Station along the Tanimachi Subway Line and Chuo Subway Line and enter through the Otemon Gate at the park's southwestern section.

❖ Special promotion:

Voyagin is an online website, which offers tours to Osaka Castle at a 20% discount. Through this promotion, a tour of Osaka Castle including the admission fee, special exhibition of turrets, and cruising program on a boat will all only cost 2700 yen. However, be sure to book early for the tour on the website as the voucher sells out pretty fast. Once booking and payment have been settled, the voucher will be sent directly to the address of your hotel for pick up. All you need to let them know is your hotel name, full name used for reservation, and check-in date. No refund will be given once the tickets have been acquired and sent to you.

❖ Things to be aware:

Osaka Castle is quite huge and has a maze-like feel to the place. Therefore, it is rather easy for you to get lost if you are a first-time visitor. Be sure to hold on to a map while you are visiting to avoid getting lost.

Recommended tips: Make sure to visit during cherry blossom season to really feel the magic of Osaka Castle. Try to make it to the castle right before sunset to take really gorgeous photos. Also, make sure to stick around for the evening hanami party. Hanami is a traditional Japanese custom of enjoying the transient beauty of flowers.

Must-See Spots in Osaka Castle:

Gokurakubashi Bridge

This is no doubt the best spot for taking photos of the Osaka Castle. From here, you can capture the bridge with the castle tower in the background. Breathtaking, isn't it?

Nishinomaru Garden

A beautiful garden around Osaka Castle. There are about 600 cherry trees here! Come in the spring and witness this whimsical view. You only need to pay 200 yen to enter this garden.

Osaka Castle Tower

❖ Opening Hours:

9 am to 5 pm. It's closed from December 28 to January 1 every year.

❖ Entrance Fee:

The park and the outer section are free, but it costs 600 yen to enter the castle tower, which now serves as a museum.

Universal Studios Japan

If you are a Potterhead like me, then this is definitely a dream come true for you. USJ is famous for its Wizarding World of Harry Potter, where you could take a stroll down Diagon Alley, and even buy your very own wand at Ollivanders. Fancy a cup of Butterbeer? Go ahead and try it for only 789 yen. Besides that, you could also see and experience a number of rides and shows, including the Flying Snoopy, Hello Kitty's Cupcake Dream, Backdraft, Space Fantasy, Jaws, Jurassic Park, and the Hollywood Dream. What are you waiting for?

❖ Opening Hours:

9 am to 9 pm every day.

❖ Entrance Fee:

7900 yen for adults and 5400 yen for children for normal passes. Express Passes allow you to skip queues for selected rides and it costs between 4,500 and 8,100 yen for four rides, and between 6,900 and 13,200 yen for seven rides. The prices may differ depending on how busy the day is.

❖ How to get there:

1) By train
✓ From Osaka Station (15 minutes, 180 yen). One direct train per hour.
✓ From Kansai Airport, take a JR airport rapid to Nishikujo Station and transfer to the JR Yumesaki Line bound for Universal City Station (75 minutes, 1190 yen).
✓ Five-minute walk from Universal City Station to the entrance of the Universal Studios Japan.

2) By bus
✓ From Kansai Airport (50-70 minutes, 1550 yen). One bus per hour.
✓ From Itami Airport (45 minutes, 930 yen). One bus per hour.

❖ Special voucher:

For USJ, I recommend using Klook.com to search for its USJ 1-day e-voucher, which will grant you entry to the theme park at 8029 yen (for adults). It is slightly more expensive than if you were to buy the entrance ticket at the ticketing counter in USJ. However, the reason I recommend this e-voucher on Klook is because it is very convenient and saves a lot of time. You don't have to queue at all to get tickets at the counter! Through Klook, once purchased, the e-voucher will be instantly sent to your email. The e-voucher sent to your email will have a bar code for you to scan upon entrance into the theme park. No queue, no hassle, and you could be the first to enter the park when it opens!

❖ Things to be aware:

Bring your sunglasses and sunblock if you wish to visit during the summer. Otherwise, you might get sunburned under the scorching heat. Wear sneakers and comfortable clothing to maximize your fun.

Recommended tips: If you wish to try out most of the rides in USJ during your visit, I recommend getting USJ Express Pass 7 because it allows you to skip the queue for 7 attractions in USJ the first time you try out the attraction. This will allow you to be able to try almost every ride in USJ at least once, and then you have to queue normally if you want to ride the attraction a second time. I also recommend you to avoid going during peak seasons and weekends because the place will be super crowded.

Dotonbori

This is one of the most interesting shopping districts in Osaka. It's bright and it looks like a giant circus. The city is filled with shopping arcades and it has an "eat all you can" culture. You can find the best Japanese shabu-shabu, crab dishes, kebabs, and sukiyaki in this area.

At the heart of the district, we have the historical Dotonbori canal. It's lined with beautiful lanterns and huge buildings. Dotonbori is, no doubt, one of the most interesting and captivating entertainment districts in Japan.

Interesting Things to do in Dotonburi:

1. Post in front of Glico's Running Man Signboard

This signboard has become so popular that everybody will know that you have been to Dotonburi once you take a picture with it. Totally insta-worthy!

2. Visit Hozenji Yokocho

Photographed by TOSHI http://blog.osakanight.com/

Home to more than 60 small izakaya, eateries and bars in an alleyway. It is located behind Hozenji Temple. It started as a theater district in the 17th century, but evolved into one of the most popular tourist spots today. If you are lucky, you may even get the chance to meet with local celebrities, as they often visit the streets of Hozenji Yokocho.

3. Enjoy the Tonbori River Cruise

There will be a guide bringing you across nine bridges where you can experience the ever-bustling Osaka at its best. You can board it in front of the "Don Quixote" discount store by the Tazaemon-bashi Bridge. The cruise will last for twenty minutes.

❖ Opening Hours:

From 1:00 PM to 9:00 PM on weekdays, 11:00 AM to 9:00 PM on Saturdays, Sundays, national holidays. Not available at 5:00 PM and 5:30 PM on weekdays.

4. Shopping at Shinsaibashi

When it comes to shopping, Osaka is arguably one of the best places to get the cheapest items. So, it's best for you to buy the things you want in Osaka instead of some other city. At Shinsaibashi-suji Shopping Arcade, there are plenty of shops lined up. This arcade offers a wide range of stores, including Zara, Uniqlo, and even luxury brands like Chanel. There is also a huge underground shopping complex here called CRYSTA, and you can find over 100 shops here!

Bonus Tips: Check out their drug stores. They are famous for selling super cheap, yet high-quality supplements. Also, be sure to catch the traditional kabuki plays at Shochikuza, which is in the heart of Dotonbori, for a taste of Japanese culture. Kabuki is a form of traditional Japanese theater effortlessly combined with dancing.

What to Eat in Osaka

1) **Takoyaki** – This is a snack made of octopus and flour. Osaka has more than 600 Takoyaki restaurants. You can eat delicious takoyakis at Ganso Takoyaki Aiduya (Price: $3 to $5) or at Dotonbori Honke Ootako ($4 to $5).

2) **Okonomiyaki** – This savory pancake is made of cabbage and flour. You can eat this delicious dish in Houzenji Sanpei (Price: $7 to $15).

3) **Negiyaki** – This looks a lot like okonomiyaki, but without the cabbage. You can find this at Yukari (Price: $7 to $15).

4) **Yakiniku** – This is a savory grilled meat dish that you can find in restaurants all over Osaka. You can eat at Yakiniku Irohakan (Average price: 3000 yen or $28)

5) **Blowfish Sashimi** – Yes, its blowfish and don't worry you won't die eating it! This dish is locally known as "tessa" and it is available in specialty stores in Osaka. You can enjoy this dish at Sushidokoro Nishiki (Price: 8300 yen or $78).

6) Japanese Curry – A type of fusion food, which has a curry flavor that originally came from India, but has been improved through the curry culture of Britain. The sauce is dark, thick and looks like brown gravy. They are usually served with udon noodles as a side dish, or some crispy pork katsu cutlet. One of the best places to try some Japanese curry is at Oretachi No Curry Ya, which is located nearby Osaka's Namba train station. (Price: A full curry plate costs 900 yen or $8)

7) Yakitori - Yakitori is a Japanese type of chicken skewers. It is prepared by skewering the meat with a type of skewer called kushi, typically made of steel, or bamboo. Afterwards, the meat is flame grilled over a charcoal fire. While the meat is grilled, it is also seasoned to perfection with tare sauce and salt. You can try this for yourself at Torikizoku, a popular Yakitori chain in Japan. (Price: Each skewer costs only 280 yen)

8) **Kappo-ryori** – This is Osaka's twist on Japanese fine dining, so the price is kind of steep but it is still worth an experience. One of the places in Osaka serving kappo-ryori is Shoubentango-tei. Over here, the cheapest course consists of five dishes determined each day by the chef. There are other longer and more expensive courses as well, but those courses require you to make a reservation beforehand. Japanese fine dining is truly an exquisite experience as the presentation of the food is just as important as the taste. You can also chat with the chef while he is intricately preparing your high-class meal with his experienced hands. Expect a budget for dinner at Shoubentango-tei to be between 8,000 yen to 9,999 yen, while lunch is between 5,000 yen to 5,999 yen.

9) **Bento** - Bento is a single-portion take-out, or home-packed meal very commonly found in Japan. A traditional bento is a box of rice or noodles, paired with fish or meat, with pickled and cooked vegetables. Just look at how cute they are! This is perfect for couples with kids that are picky eaters, as no kid will be able to resist feasting on these. You can easily find many different types of these boxed meals at supermarkets. Each box will only cost about 1000 yen.

10) Shokudo – Shokudo are casual restaurants, or cafeterias that serve a variety of reasonably-priced Japanese dishes. From noodle dishes like udon, ramen, and soba to rice dishes like donburi and curry rice, they have it all. Set meals can also be found here and they include main dishes such as grilled fish, sashimi or tempura that are served with a bowl of rice, miso soup and pickles. A meal here will cost around 500 to 1500 yen. A bonus here is that the tea is free!

Where to Stay in Osaka

Kita is the best area to stay for first-time tourists. It's the business center of the city. You could find a lot of hotels in the area, including:

1. **Imperial Hotel Osaka** – If you have money to spare, stay in the Imperial Hotel Osaka. It's the best luxury hotel located at the heart of Kita. It's just a short walk from JR Sakuranomiya Station and JR Osaka Station.

2. **S. Training Hotel** – This is a mid-range hotel. Rooms come with private bathrooms, TV, and even an electronic kettle. Priced at $115 per night.

3. **Hostel Tankai** – This hostel is best for those who have a tight budget. Staying in this hostel will give you a chance to meet new people, too. Prices start at $18 per night.

There are also cheaper options like capsule hotels and comic book cafes if you do not wish to stay at hotels.

4. **Capsule Hotel Asahi Plaza Shinsaibashi** – Capsule hotels are a bit pricier than hostels, but they are still cheaper than hotel rooms. A night here will cost around 3000 yen. Capsule hotels are clean, comfy, and offer you privacy throughout the night.

5. **Manga Kissa** – Love to read comic books, sip a cup of tea, and spin around on a big, comfy chair? You can do just that at this comic book café, as it is open all night. This café offers lodging (1500 yen for 8 hours) which is perfect if you want to just read through the night until you fall asleep on the chair. Pillows and blankets are also provided if you wish to sleep on the floor till morning.

6. **Osaka Hana Hostel** – This is also a great choice if you are on a budget trip. Located in the heart of Amerika-Mura, this hostel has plenty of rooms for you to choose from. From six-bed dorms to Japanese style rooms and Western style rooms, there is sure to be a room that is to your liking. Some of the facilities include coin laundry machines, kitchen and lounge areas. The staff are also friendly and speak good English.

Recommendation: If you are on a budget trip, you may also check out Airbnb.com to find the cheapest accommodation best suited to your liking. On that website, you can find hundreds of hosts willing to let you stay at their accommodation at a decent price. They provide pictures of the rooms, bathrooms and facilities for you to check out before you make a booking. The facilities they provide include washing machines and dryers. Also, every accommodation on the website has its own ratings, reviews, and comments of the place for you to look at.

Side Trip: The Deer Paradise Called Nara

(Suggested Time – One Day)

Nara was once the capital of Japan before it was transferred to Kyoto. Therefore, you can easily find ancient structures around the city. What's most fascinating about Nara is that you can find deer everywhere and they're very comfortable around humans. This city is also just 39 minutes away from Osaka.

You can simply take a train from Osaka or Tokyo to Kintetsu Nara Station (not Nara Station).

Recommended tips: If you do not wish to hassle yourself looking around for transportation, I recommend using Trip Advisor to search for tours in Nara. You will be able to find quite a few offering afternoon and morning tours of Todaiji Temple, Deer Park and Kasuga Shrine. Most of the Nara tours on Trip Advisor also include a trip to Kyoto! The good thing about a tour is that you can save time planning your journey and waiting for public transport. Instead, you can just enjoy a well-planned itinerary. You can also choose to include food in the tour package if you wish.

Places you must visit at least once in Nara:

#1 Nara Deer Park

If you like to play with deers and love Bambi, you should head to Nara Park. It also has plenty of cherry trees that bloom during the springtime. They have a large population of semi-wild deer roaming freely around the park.

You can buy a pack of deer crackers for about 300yen (shika sembei) to feed them. Never feed them your own food.

❖ How to get there:

100 meters from Kintetsu Nara Station

❖ Opening Hours:

This park is open 24 hours a day

❖ Entrance fee:

Free

Caution: Note that the deer can be very aggressive in trying to get the crackers out of your hands. Also, when they sense that you have the crackers, they will swarm toward you uncontrollably. How cute!

#2 Kasuga-taisha Shrine

Kasuga-Taisha Shrine is the most important Shinto shrine in Nara. It consists of pathways lined with thousands of stone lanterns, surrounded by a zen-like forest and of course the deer, roaming happily and freely.

❖ Opening Hours:

6:00am-6:00pm (Apr-Sep)

6:30am-5:00pm (Oct-Mar)

❖ Nearest Transport:

25min walk from Kintetsu Nara Station

❖ Entrance fee:

Free. You may need to pay if you want to enter the temple inner section.

Bonus tips: Come and experience the magical Mantoro festival on Feb 3rd and Aug 14th. During this festival, all the 3000 lanterns will be lit.

#3 Todaiji Temple

Todaiji Temple is a towering Buddhist temple and it is the home of Daibutsu, the biggest bronze Buddha statue in the world! Even though the temple is busy during weekdays, it still feels holy and sacred. There's something about this temple that just transports you to ancient Japan. So just open your mind and heart, and let the temple take you on a transient, tranquil journey of self-discovery. Also, don't forget to check out the Nandai-mon Gate as well.

❖ Fun-fact:

This temple is certified as a UNESCO World Heritage Site due to its rich history.

❖ Opening Hours:

7:30am-5:30pm (Apr-Oct), 8:00am-4:30pm (Nov-Mar)

❖ Nearest Transport:

20min walk from Kintetsu Nara Station

❖ Entrance fee:

Free for the outer section. 500yen for the inner section.

#4 Yoshikien - Nara's great little secrets

Yoshikien is a park with three gardens – a moss garden, a tea ceremony garden, and a pond garden. As you can see from the picture, it looks like a setting straight out of a Disney movie! Such is the beauty and magic that this park has to offer. Whether it is a lovely, romantic stroll, or a tea party and picnic, this garden is peaceful and relaxing enough for you to enjoy spending your leisure time here. It is located directly next to Isui-en Garden.

❖ Opening Hours:

9:00am-5:00pm (enter by 4:30pm). It's closed every Feb 15 to Feb 28

❖ Nearest Transport:

15min walk from Kintetsu Nara Station

❖ Entrance fee:

250 yen but it's free for foreigners.

Bonus tip: The maple trees here are spectacular in November. Straight out of a fairytale.

➤ You may be wondering why is there so little information about Nara especially when there are so much more other temples available? It's because I have chosen only the best destinations for your maximum experience in the shortest time possible. The rest of the temples are about the same and they are less attractive when compared to those mentioned above. So, you may want to skip them if you don't have much time.

Nara's Transportation:

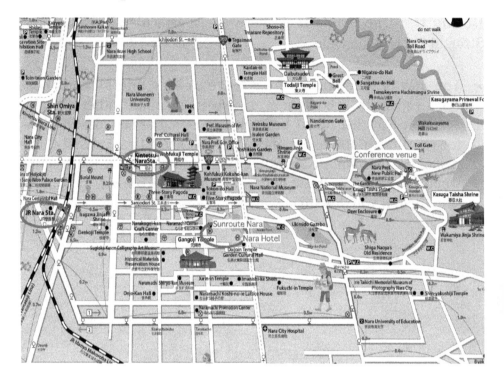

Take the 100yen bus to all the tourist sites.

You can find its bus stop right in front of the Kintetsu Nara Station.

You will need to pay 100yen when you enter the bus every single time. If you are going to four destinations, that means you will have to pay 400yen.

Chapter 6 - Hokkaido: The Land of Beer, Music Boxes, and Colorful Landscapes

Hokkaido, formerly known as Ezo, or Yesso, is the second biggest island in Japan. The scenery is spectacular, the air is crisp, and the waters are crystal clear. Although the cities in Hokkaido are not as popular as Tokyo, Osaka, or Kyoto, they're just as wonderful and breathtakingly beautiful. Therefore, it is a must to visit Hokkaido at least once in your lifetime. The whole island looks like a scenic wallpaper, especially during the summer and winter. Filled with rainbow-colored landscapes and the home to many natural wonders in Japan, Hokkaido is truly a paradise of nature.

Places to See in Hokkaido

Hokkaido looks like a tropical haven of flora and fauna during the summertime and a stunning kingdom of ice and snow during the winter season. It's also filled with vibrant colors during the spring and fall season.

Sapporo (Suggested Time – Two to three days)

Sapporo is the capital of Hokkaido and home to one of the most famous beers in Japan. But, there's more to Sapporo than just the beer. It's a modern city that's filled with rare sights and things to do. Basically, it is an Eastern city, but with a strong European vibe to it. Be it a booming food scene, chic cafes, glitzy nightlife, or a plethora of shopping places, you name it, Sapporo has it.

Here's a list of places that you should visit when you're in Sapporo:

1. Odori Park

It is located at the center of Sapporo, separating the northern and the southern part of the city. This park is about one kilometer and a half long, stretching over twelve city blocks. Unlike other parks, it is especially calm and peaceful here, perfect for relaxing and clearing your mind. Many locals visit this park just to take a break and unwind themselves. There are lots of events being held here throughout the year. For example, the Snow Festival in winter, Lilac Festival in spring, YOSAKOI Soran Festival and beer garden in summer, and Autumn Fest during fall.

❖ How to get there:

The best way to get there is by walking. You can walk there through the underground shopping street, where you can experience the taste and culture of Hokkaido. It's a 1.5-kilometer walk from Sapporo Station, but you will be there in no time at all as you stroll through, while enjoying the beautiful sights. Just look out for their huge and easily spotted Odori Park signboards.

❖ Entrance Fee:

Free

❖ Opening Hours:

24 hours

❖ Best time to visit:

Spring.
In the spring, you can just wear a normal layer of clothes, and feel the gentle breeze softly brushing your face as you leisurely stroll around the park. Early February during winter, the park serves as the main site of the Sapporo Snow Festival.

Meet the Sapporo TV Tower – The Landmark of Sapporo

This tower was built two years before Tokyo Tower, around 1956 when the wave of a new era of television technology washed by Japan. It has an observation deck at a height of 90 meters, where you can enjoy the stunning view of the park and surrounding cities.

Sapporo TV Tower has a height of 147.2 meters and will be illuminated during the evening. You can just view the tower from below. There is no need for you to visit its observation deck if you have already visited Tokyo Tower, or Tokyo Skytree.

❖ Opening hours:

9:00 to 22:00 (late April to mid-October)

9:30 to 21:30 (mid-October to late April)

❖ Entrance Fee:

720 yen

Recommendations: Klook offers a voucher to visit this tower at only 665 yen. All you have to do is book beforehand and pay by credit card. The voucher will then be immediately sent to your email upon payment. This will also help you save time as you do not need to queue up to buy the entry ticket on the day you visit.

2. Former Hokkaido Government Office – The Red Brick Office

This orange, baroque building used to be the seat of power in Hokkaido and was used for approximately 80 years until the new government office currently in use was built. The building is surrounded by colorful gardens and illuminates at night.

Are you a history enthusiast? Do you love finding out about the true stories behind olden architectures and how they came to exist? If you answer yes to both those questions, then this is the place for you! Here, you will be able to know more about Japan's rich political history as there are plenty of historical exhibits around for you to look at and learn from. There are also shows from local Japanese artists inside the building.

❖ Opening Hours:

8:45-18:00. Closed on New Year's holidays.

❖ Entrance Fee:

Free

❖ How to get there:

It is located at the west of Kita Sanjo Dori. You will notice it while on your way to the Odori Park. If can also get there by subway as well. It's an 8-minute walk from west exit of JR Sapporo Station or 4-minute walk from Exit 10 of Sapporo Station (Namboku and Toho subway lines)

❖ Best time to visit:

Spring season (around May~June). There will be all kinds of flowers in full bloom across the Government Office during this season.

Bonus Tip: Request for a volunteer staff for explanations about the building to appreciate its depth. English, Chinese (Simplified/Traditional), Korean, Thai are available.

3. Mount Moiwa Observation Deck - Sacred Places for Love

This is the perfect romantic spot for lovers all around. Just look at how dreamy it is in the picture! Under the moonlit sky, you and your significant other are guaranteed to fall deeper in love with each other on this deck overlooking the bright city lights of Japan.

There is a mini cable car available to lift you all the way up to the summit. From there, you can see the whole city from the observation deck. There's also plenty of restaurants, a planetarium and a theater at the upper station. You are sure to impress your date by bringing them here.

On the mountain's southeastern side, there is the Mount Moiwa Ski Resort. However, it is not connected to the Mount Moiwa Ropeway. So, you will need to approach it from a different location.

You could also find the "bell of happiness" in the area. Legend says that couples who lock a padlock and ring the bell here will find eternal and everlasting happiness.

❖ Entrance fee:

1700 yen (roundtrip for ropeway and mini cable car)

1100 yen (roundtrip for ropeway only)

600 yen (roundtrip for mini cable car only)

700 yen for adults and 500 yen for children

❖ Opening Hours:

10:30 to 22:00 (from 11:00 from December to March); admission ends 30 minutes before closing.

❖ How to get there:

Take Sapporo streetcar line to Ropeway Iriguchi station from Susukino (cost about 170 yen and 25 minutes). Once you arrived, take a free shuttle bus to the lower part of the ropeway station.

Bonus Tip: Make sure to come around, or after sunset to truly be blown away by the view.

4. Moerenuma Park

Moerenuma Park is unlike anything you've ever seen. It is the perfect blend of nature mixed in with creative genius at the best location outside the concrete jungles of Sapporo. Make sure to spend a few hours here if you're in Sapporo.

This glass museum looks a lot like the Pyramid in Paris, France. It's located in the beautiful Moerenuma Park in Higashi-ku.

The park was designed by Isamu Noguchi, a renowned Japanese American sculptor. Noguchi was born in the United States, but spent most of his life in Japan. This area was initially a waste disposal site before it was transformed into this gorgeous park.

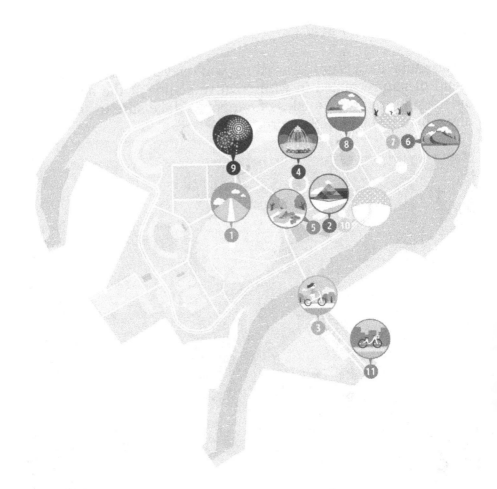

❖ Must-do list for visitors at Moerenuma Park:

1. Climb the 62-meter tall Mt. Moere

2. Visit the glass pyramid "Hiidamari"

3. Rent and ride a bike around the park

4. Watch the fountain water spout show

5. Have a small picnic

6. Play with the art facilities specially designed by Isamu Noguchi

7. Enjoy the cherry trees in the spring

8. Get wet in the water at Moere Beach in the summer

9. Watch the grand firework show in the fall

10. Slide around using rented sleds or ski in the winter

❖ How to get there:

Take the Toho Subway Line to Kanjodori-higashi Station and then change to local bus number 69 or 79 to the park's east entrance. The name of the bus stop you are supposed to drop by is Moerenuma Koen Higashi-guchi, モエレ沼公園東口. The journey will cost 210 yen, and 25 minutes not including the waiting time. There are usually 2 buses per hour.

❖ Entrance Fees:

Free

❖ Opening Hours:

East Entrance Gate: 7:00 - 22:00 (admission till 21:00)

*Open every day

Bonus Tip: Bring along some snacks, sandwiches and drinks with you for a picnic in case you get hungry because there are no snack shops nearby, only restaurants.

5. Sapporo Beer Museum

The Germans introduced beer in Japan in 1860 and the Japanese have been obsessed with this alcoholic beverage ever since. If you're into beer, you should definitely visit the Sapporo Beer Museum for a new experience. At Sapporo Beer Museum, you can witness the process of beer making and understand the history of beer in Japan. Remember to also visit the Tasting Lounge on the 1st floor, where you can taste a wide variety of beer at a small fee (200 yen to 300 yen). Options of beer available for tasting include Sapporo's signature Black Label, Sapporo Classic, as well as Kaitakushi Pilsner, all of which are found only in Hokkaido.

Bonus Tip: You do not need to sign up for an English tour here, as there are English explanations all around the museum for you to understand easily.

6. The Sapporo Beer Garden

Located right next to the Sapporo Beer Museum. Besides the grand beer halls, you can also find quite a few all-you-can-drink beers and all-you-can-eat BBQ also known as Jingisukan restaurants (which you can only find in Hokkaido).

❖ How to get there:

Take the "Loop 88 Factory Line" bus that stops at places like Odori Station and Seibu department store near Sapporo Station. The bus departures every 20 minutes and cost 210 yen per ride. You can also walk there from JR Sapporo Station which takes about 25 minutes or 15 minutes from Higashi-kuyakusho-mae Station on the Toho Subway Line.

❖ Entrance Fees:

Free. Guided tour for 500 yen.

❖ Opening Hours:

11:30 to 20:00 (last admission until 19:30). Closed on Mondays and New Year's holidays.

Otaru (Suggested Time – One day)

Otaru is a scenic port city. It is known for its beautiful landscapes, music boxes, and old-fashioned sake brewery. You can see glass and pastel-colored buildings everywhere you look. Here's a list of places that you should see in Otaru:

1. Otaru Canal

There's something soft and romantic about this canal. It has a dreamy and nostalgic feel to its atmosphere. It was built in 1923 to allow small boats to transport cargo. However, it has not been used as a docking facility since the 1980s. The canal is lined with old warehouses that are now used as museums, cafés, and shops. The 63 elegant gas lamps will light up the area at night, creating the perfect romantic atmosphere for a lovely night stroll under the stars.

In the winter, Snow Light Path Festival is held here.

❖ How to get there:

The Otaru Canal is a ten-minute walk from Otaru Station. Once you have exited the station, keep walking towards the north and you will find it in no time.

2. Saikaimachi Dori Street

This is a quaint, little street that is well known for its glass products. You can find the Music Box Museum in this area. Besides that, you can also visit different shops around the area that sell cakes and chocolate potato chips.

❖ Don't miss these best spots:

Music Box Museum

This is the largest music box museum in the world! It features glass sculptures and glass music boxes built with the very essence of Otaru's uniqueness. They have more than 30,000 music boxes for you to choose from, each with its own different design and music to suit your taste. The price for each music box also varies depending on its size and design.

As you can see in the picture above, this place is a little slice of magic, which will make you feel like you are stepping into Santa's workshop. It would be lovely to buy and keep a music box as a souvenir from your trip.

- ❖ Opening Hours: 9:00 to 18:00 (until 19:00 on Fridays and Saturdays in summer). Open every day.
- ❖ Entrance Fee: Free

Museum of Venetian Art

His art gallery was opened, for the purpose of bringing the richness and elegance of the ancient city of Venice to Otaru. You can admire all of his artworks here.

- ❖ Opening Hours: 8:45 to 18:00 (entry until 17:30). Open every day.
- ❖ Entrance Fee: 700 yen

LeTAO Main Store

You can buy various type of sweets that are purely made from Hokkaido ingredients. Don't forget to check out their ever-popular Baumkuchen, which is a ring-shaped traditional German layer cake.

- ❖ Opening Hours: 10:00 - 18:00. The cafe closes 30 minutes before the end for business hours. Open every day.
- ❖ Entrance Fee: 700 yen

Kitaichi Outlet

You can buy high-quality Kitaichi Glass products at a reasonable price here.

- ❖ Opening Hours: 8:45am-6:00pm (Close)
- ❖ Prices: Glasses from 750 yen/Bowls from 500 yen/Soy sauce cruets from 1100 yen

3. Sankaku Fish Market

This is just a few steps away from the JR Otaru station. You could find a great bargain on rare fishes and huge crabs. The market opens from 8 am to 5 pm every day.

Furano-Biei (Suggested Time – Two days)

Furano (富良野) and Biei (美瑛) are located right in the heart of Hokkaido. They are most well-known for their natural wonders ranging from calming lavender fields to the bluest ponds during summer and cross-country skis during winter.

The best time to visit: July~August, when all their flowers and lavenders are fully bloomed.

Bonus Tips: If you come to the Furano-Biei area by airplane, consider booking a flight to Sapporo instead of Asahikawa even though Asahikawa Airport is nearer. Buying your flight ticket to Sapporo will cost you much lesser when combined. Once you arrived, buy the JR Furano-Biei Free Ticket which costs 6,500 yen for adults and 3,250 yen for children at Shin-Chitose Airport JR Station. You can use the Free Ticket in Asahikawa, Takigawa, Furano, and Biei as many times as you wish up to four days.

Furano

#1 Farm Tomita

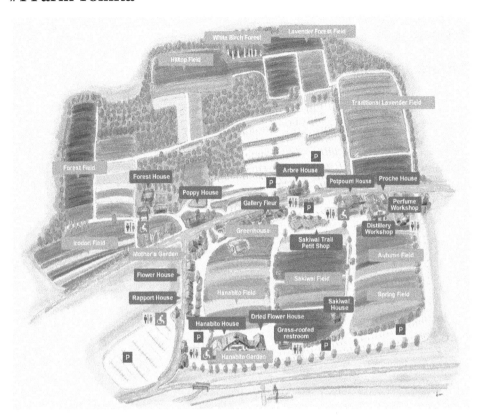

Farm Tomita is located in Nakafurano and is the most popular lavender field in Japan. The farm looks like a rainbow as it is covered in so many different colors during the spring and summer months. It is so beautiful that you will be at a loss for words. The flower beds are neatly lined up to form a vast rainbow-like field.

❖ When to visit:

Last week of July to August when all the flowers are in full bloom.

❖ How to get there:

Take the train and get off at 'Lavender Field Station' on the JR Furano Line. The Lavender Field Station is not always open. If it is closed, you will need to get off at Nakafurano Station and walk to Farm Tomita.

❖ Entrance Fee:

Free

❖ Opening Hours:

The farm is open from 8:30 am to 5 pm.

#2 Municipal Lavender Field

During the summer, Furano Ski Area will transform into a picturesque Lavender field. Hokusei Hill will be naturally carpeted in purple. Use the elevator which cost about 200 yen to get to the best view on top.

❖ How to get there:

10-minute walk from JR Naka-Furano station

❖ Opening Hours:

From 9:00 a.m. to 4:40 p.m., June～August

Address: 〒071-0714 Nakafurano, Miyamachi 1-41

Tel: +81-167-44-2123

Biei

There are a few sightseeing buses here offering to bring you to the top destinations in Biei because most of the destinations are quite far apart. So, walking is no longer an option. My recommendation is to just go ahead and book for these sightseeing buses.

IMPORTANT! Make sure to book your seat a few days before your Biei trip. You really don't want to be disappointed. You can buy these tickets at any major train station in Hokkaido. Just simply grab them once you arrive in Sapporo.

It's not possible for you to book online.

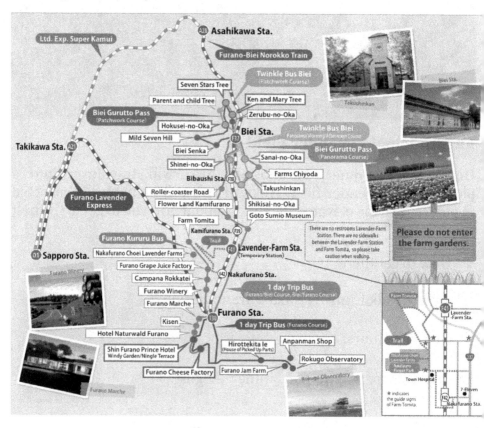

Here's a map for the sightseeing bus tours available during summer (July-August)

**Please beware that bus schedule and courses will change according to seasons.

Here's a list of the best destinations in Biei: (They are all covered by the sightseeing buses)

#1 Shirogane Blue Pond

Shirogane Blue Pond in winter

Note: The pond sometimes freezes during winter and when it freezes you don't get to see the bluish-colored pond. Everything turns white as ice. The pond is part of an initiative to protect the town of Biei in case of an eruption by Mount Takachidake.

You may be wondering why the pond is so blue? Well, it turns out that the color is a result of colloidal aluminum hydroxide present in the water.

#2 Shikisai.no.Oka

Shikisai.no.Oka is a 15-hectare hill blanketed by all types of colorful flowers from April to October. There will be different flowers according to the seasons with July-August being the peak. You can find flowers such as salvia, Japanese anemone, sunflower, tulip, lavender, dahlia lupine and way more.

❖ There is a tractor bus service available for those who do not wish to walk. The vehicle will bring you around the hill to take in the beauty of nature.

✓ Time Required: 15 minutes

✓ Fare:

300 yen for elementary school and junior high school students
500 yen for high school students or more

#3 Hokusei-no-Oka View Park

The pyramid-shaped observation deck overlooking the majestic Tokachi mountain.

There are souvenir shops, tourist information center and studio glass here as well.

#4 Ken and Mary Tree

Ken and Mary Tree (ケンとメリーの木) is a huge poplar tree located in Biei at the southeastern part of Asahikawa city. It is easy to spot this tree because it grows tall on a gentle hillside. This tree was used as a shooting location for a television commercial, which was broadcasted in 1976, and the tree was named after the characters in the commercial.

#5 Seven Stars Tree (view from the bus)

The Seven Stars Tree became viral overnight after its image was used on a box of Seven Star cigarettes. Since then, people have flocked over to take in this scenic spot that manages to capture the scenery of the hills of Biei.

#3 Parent and Child Tree (view from the bus)

The two oak trees standing in between a smaller tree symbolizes the parent whereas the smaller tree symbolizes the child. Together, they stand strong and proud, not giving in to the brutality of nature.

Where to Stay in Hokkaido

1) **SappoLodge** – A rustic cabin hidden in the heart of Susukino, Sapporo, the perfect choice for any adventurer looking for a pleasant stay. The concept is quite unique and there is even a climbing wall for you to use instead of stairs. Youngsters who plan on backpacking Japan should definitely check this place out. The host of this accommodation also considers himself quite the adventurer, with over 14 years of experience as a guide, so he will be able to recommend to you all of his best hiking locations if you are interested.

Bonus Tip: Prices here are subject to change every day. So, I highly recommend you to visit booking.com to survey the prices in advance before your trip. The prince range will roughly be around 3000 yen to 8000 yen.

2) Nakamuraya Ryokan — As Japanese as the name of this place is, that's how traditional and rich in Japanese culture this place is. It is located just a stone's throw away from the entrance to the Hokkaido University Botanical Garden, which is around 10 minutes from JR Sapporo Station by walking. This Japanese-style inn is perfect for those who want to truly get a taste of Japanese culture as travelers who stay here will sleep on tatami floors (rush-covered straw mat) using futons (traditional Japanese bedding). There is also a communal bath called o-furo for you to relax and soak away all your fatigue from the day.

Bonus Tip: You may also request for meals upon booking if you wish. Do not worry if you do not speak Japanese, as the hosts here are friendly and very much used to foreign travelers. Don't hesitate to ask them if you have any inquiries.

3) Moiwa Lodge 834 — This is the one and only ski-in, ski-out capsule hotel in the world. Located in front of the Moiwa lifts, it is perfect for those who love to ski and want to stay as near as possible to the ski resort in Niseko. You do not have to worry about your ski gear either as this lodge provides you with plenty of safe space to keep them. However, note that this capsule hotel separates its rooms by gender. There are buffet meals too for you to devour at the comfy lounge, which overlooks the snowy mountains. The hotel also does free pick-ups from the Kanronomori bus stop.

4) Morinoki – If you wish to stay in Otaru, this is a very good choice for you. The must-see sights in Otaru are not that many and can generally be visited all in one day, but it is still a beautiful neighborhood to stay at if you wish. Morinoki is a nice little backpackers hostel, which is perfect for a short duration of stay during your trip. The staff can speak multiple languages, the facilities are intact, and the lounge areas are super relaxing. You can also order meals here that are very decently priced at only 390 yen (breakfast) and 500 yen (dinner). You can find this little hostel by walking 15 minutes from JR Otaru Station.

5) JR Tower Hotel Nikko Sapporo – If you are planning on splurging on this trip, go ahead and book your room at this posh hotel. You will be able to feel like a prince or princess by staying here. From the luxurious hotel rooms to the most top-notch room service, everything will be to your satisfaction. It is located right on top of JR Sapporo Station, which is very convenient for you to travel around Sapporo. There is also a relaxing hot spring for you to immerse in for an extra 1600 won. Go ahead and pamper yourself here if you wish because you deserve it.

What to Eat in Hokkaido

What better way to experience a culture than to literally taste it? From the freshest seafood to flower-flavored ice cream, Hokkaido is no stranger to exquisite cuisine. Hokkaido is known for its dairy products such as its butter and cream and it also offers a wide variety of food guaranteed to make you drool. These are some of the food that you have to try if you visit.

1) **Menya Saimi** – Ask the locals and you will know that this ramen shop is arguably one of the very best in Hokkaido, if not even the country. Hence, the queue will no doubt be long, but once you taste the first mouthful of a hot, steaming bowl of miso ramen here, all the waiting would have been worth it. Bonus, it isn't even that expensive! If you are a ramen lover, don't think twice and just go to this place.

2) **Kani-honke** – The king of crabs makes an appearance at this place, and so should you! Hokkaido is famous for its seafood, and what screams seafood more than tasty crabs? The kani-suki here costs 4400 yen per person and it is similar to sukiyaki, except crab is added into the hot pot. Crab, vegetables, rice, and egg are all boiled in a delicious seafood broth for you to savor. There is a huge crab sign on the building, so you can easily spot this place. There is also a branch of this place near the Susukino crossing.

3) **Jingisukan** – Charcoal-grilled mutton which is considered a legacy of Hokkaido's rich history of the sheep-rearing program in the 19th century. The name Jinisukan is actually a Japanese take from the name Genghis Khan, Japan's very own warrior. It is named as such because of the shape of the cast-iron hotplate used when grilling the meat, which is said to resemble the warrior's helmet. Pair this sensational meat with some beer and enjoy the combination of flavors dancing in your mouth.

4) **Ainu cuisine** – Ainu is a type of ethnic in Japan and their cuisine is special in its own way. Unfortunately, not much is left of one of Hokkaido's most indigenous cuisine. Only a few restaurants serving Ainu cuisine is scattered across Sapporo and in Akan National Park. Some of this cuisine include ruibe (raw, frozen salmon sliced up like sashimi) which is dipped in some soy sauce. Ainu cuisine also has pocche, which are traditional dumplings made from potato mash, salmon soup and some vegetables. If you are keen to try some special cuisine only found in Hokkaido, go ahead and try it for yourself.

5) **Butadon** – Butadon literally means a bowl of pork and rice. Large slices of marinated pork that taste sweet and savory are generously topped on a bowl of steaming rice. The sauce is rich, the meat of the pork is tender and juicy, and the flavors all work really well with the rice. Also, this dish is rich in protein and vitamin, which can help you regain your energy after a tiring day. In Hokkaido, you can try a bowl of heavenly Butadon at Ippin. They are famous for their bowls of Butadon and Ippin is a franchise with 5 branches in Sapporo, and its original shop in Obihiro city.

6) **Shiroi koibito** - Shiroi Koibito (white lover) is a famous cookie made by Japanese confectionery maker Ishiya in Sapporo. These delicious and beautifully packed boxes of white chocolate cookies make the perfect gifts and souvenirs from your trip. As you bite into the thin, crispy, French-styled langue de chat cookies, the richness of the white chocolate and the cookie will melt in your mouth and make you feel happy with every bite. There is a reason why Shiroi koibito is so famous throughout Hokkaido, so go ahead and try it for yourself and you will know why. A box of Shiroi koibito will cost you 700 yen (12-pack) and 1400 yen (24-pack).

Chapter 7 - Winter Destinations

Japan feels like a tropical paradise during the summer, and it is completely magical during the winter season. If you decide to visit Japan during winter, here's a list of sites that you should visit:

Shirakawago

Want to know what it feels like walking in a winter wonderland? Go ahead and pay a visit to Shirakawago, a village located in Gifu. It is known for its Gassho-zukuris or thatched houses that look a lot like English cottages, or gingerbread houses. These cottages look magical when they're covered with snow and light up doing the winter season. The village literally looks like the perfect Christmas movie scene.

You'll be able to see the whole village light up during the last two Sundays of January and the first two Sundays of February.

Did you know? – In December 1995, the Historic Villages of Shirakawa-go and Gokayama were added to the list of UNESCO World Heritage sites.

Recommendations: Try their beef BBQ and chocolate ice cream here, it's wonderful!

Zao Snow Monsters

Zao Onsen is a popular hot spring and ski resort in the Yamagata Prefecture. It's a ski hub and a haven for those who want to stay warm during the winter season. It has scenic landscapes during the summer and spring seasons. It also looks super mysterious and intriguing during the winter season.

The Snow Monsters look like well-crafted ice sculptures from afar. But, they're actually just natural wonders. They're merely snow-covered trees that form cool monster-like shapes. Aren't they the coolest? See what I just did there?

Bonus Tip: The snow monsters are visible at the peak of the Zao Ski Resort, and they look the best around mid-February. You can access the monsters using a ropeway, or a gondola for both skiers and non-skiers.

The hot spring fee ranges from 300 yen to 1500 yen.

❖ Entrance fees:

200 yen.

❖ Ski resort Opening Hours:

6 am to 10 pm.

Zao Onsen Ski Resort features long runs with good snow, many slopes for all skill levels, and the famous snow monsters.

Season*

First snow to early May

Lifts

32 lifts

Tickets

Full day - 5000 yen

Half day - 4000 yen

Nighter - 2000 yen

Access

40 minutes by bus or car from Yamagata Station.

* Season dates may be adjusted due to lack of snow. Check

before going.

Jigokudani Monkey Park

Jigokudani Monkey Park is the home of the snow monkeys. It's part of the Shigakogen, or Joshinetsu Kogen National Park. It was called Hell's Valley because of its natural boiling pool of water that's surrounded by tall cliffs and cold forests.

This park was founded in 1964 and has since become the home of red-faced Japanese Macaques, or Snow Monkeys. This is the only place in the world where you can see monkeys enjoy bathing in hot water. This park gives the visitors a unique experience of bathing in hot steam during the cold winter season. Having already been accustomed to humans, the monkeys can be observed pretty close and they will still completely ignore you. Naturally, it is not allowed to touch or feed the monkeys.

❖ Entrance Fee:

500 yen.

❖ Opening Hours:

Open from 8:30 am to 5:00 pm during the spring and summer seasons. It is open from 9 am to 4 pm during the autumn and winter seasons.

❖ How to get there:

There are two ways to get to the Monkey Park, the first way requires a 25-40-minute walk through the forest, and the other way requires a 10-15-minute walk from the nearest parking lot.

✓ The first way involves taking a bus to Kanbayashi Onsen from Yudanaka Station (10-15 minutes, 310 yen, 1-2 buses per hour), Shibu Onsen (5-10 minutes, 190 yen, 1-2 buses per hour) or Nagano Station (40 minutes, 1400 yen, 4-10 buses per day).

The buses along the Yudanaka-Kanbayashi Line will stop at "Kanbayashi Onsen" bus stop, while all the other buses stop at the "Snow Monkey Park" bus stop, only a short walk away.

If you are feeling more adventurous, you can go from Kanbayashi Onsen, which is a 30-40-minute walk to the monkey park. The walking trail is passable around the year, but be sure to use sturdy footwear especially in winter.

✓ The second way involves a 10-15-minute walk from a paid parking lot right to the west of the monkey park. However, the narrow road from Shibu Onsen to the parking lot is not accessible by public transportation and gets closed during winter. It is rather time-consuming, but still possible to walk to the parking lot from Shibu Onsen in about 45-60 minutes when it isn't snowing.

Some accommodations in Yudanaka and Shibu offer their guests free rides to the parking lot.

Sapporo Snow Festival

Sapporo Winter Festival usually happens during the first week of February and it boasts some of the biggest snow sculptures in Japan. You can find giant sculptures, snowmobile rides, and even snow slides there. There are even Pokemon or Super Mario sculptures for you to see. The admission fee is free and the booths are open from 9 am to 9 pm for three consecutive days.

Otaru Snow Light Path

The Otaru Snow Light Path happens during the first week of February and ends during the second week of February.

This festival happens in the beautiful city of Otaru, also known as the "Wall Street of the North". During the ten-day festival, certain parts of the city (the Temiyasen Kaijo and Unga Kaijo) are filled with glittering lanterns, shimmering lights, small ice sculptures, and candlelight. The festival sites also offer the best Otaru delicacies, such as the Otaru sushi, seafood, beer, wine, mochi, and ramen. If you decide to witness this snow festival, you can stay in some of the recommended hotels near the Otaru Station and the Otaru canal, namely:

✓ **Authent Hotel Otaru**

✓ **Hotel Sonia**

✓ **Smile Hotel**

✓ **Otaru Furukawa**

Chapter 8 – Kyushu: The Land of Fire

Kyushu, literally meaning nine provinces, is Japan's third largest island. Located southwest of the main island, it has a sub-tropical climate. This vast countryside is a paradise for travelers to get off the beaten track and see the unseen Japan.

In Kyushu, you can find active volcanoes, beautiful waterfalls, natural hot springs and pristine beaches.

Fukuoka serves as the gateway to Kyushu. As a popular metropolis, it has delicious street food and bustling nightlife. Meanwhile, the picturesque Nagasaki is a shining example of regrowth and hope. With its wonderful nature and unique culture, Kyushu will leave a deep impression in your mind.

Consider renting a car in Kyushu as you might waste quite some time if you only rely on public transportation.

Prefectures
❖ Fukuoka
❖ Kagoshima
❖ Saga
❖ Oita
❖ Miyazaki
❖ Nagasaki
❖ Kumamoto

Bonus Tip: There are discounted all-you-can-ride passes on JR Kyushu and Kyushu buses, from 8000 yen/10,000 yen for 3 days in northern Kyushu/all of Kyushu, or a four-day all-Kyushu Pass for 14,000 yen. For further information, visit www.sunqpass.jp.

Fukuoka

Fukuoka is the largest city in Kyushu. It is particularly popular for its Hakata *tonkotsu* ramen and *motsunabe* (stew made with beef or pork offal and vegetables).

Walk along Naka River in Nakasu District in the evening, and you will find a long line of *yatai* (small stalls). Immerse in the one-of-a-kind atmosphere that you will hardly find in other places in Japan nowadays. You can also find some yatai around Tenjin station that sells authentic food at a reasonable price. Do note that most of these stalls are closed on rainy days.

Fukuoka also has a few shopping centers that are great to explore. One of them is Fukuoka Canal City, which has a music fountain. Another one is Tenjin Underground Shopping Centre that is just a stone's throw away from the train station.

If you want to relax after hectic sightseeing, go to Ohori Park. At Ohorikoen subway station, take Exit 3 and walk straight. After that, turn left and you will see the beautiful park. You can have a picnic here, or just take a quiet, nice stroll. There is also a Starbucks located in the park.

Bonus Tip: Hakata Gion Yamakasa Festival is held during the first two weeks of July. On 15 July, there is a 5-km race in which the participating groups compete with each other, while carrying the huge portable shrines called *yamakasa*. It is an exciting event not to be missed.

Dazaifu

It has a cluster of temples, a famous shrine and a national museum, making for a popular day trip from Fukuoka. It is located 16km away from Tenjin Station, so you can just catch a train to get there.

Once you have arrived at Dazaifu Station, you will be in central Dazaifu. The main attractions, namely Tenmangu Shrine, Kyushu National Museum and Komyozen-ji are all within walking distance.

Try the local specialty, *umegae*-mochi, which is filled with sweet azuki bean paste and imprinted with plum flowers. Go for the stall that is far inside the walking street and look out for where the locals queue up.

❖ How to get there:

Take a train from Tenjin Station to Dazaifu Station (400 yen each way, 25 minutes). Alternatively, take a direct bus at Hakata Station.

❖ The main attractions here:

1. Tenmangu Shrine

Being deified as Tenman Tenjin, the poet scholar Sugawara-no-Michizane is the god of culture and scholars to the locals. Many students come to this place to pray for academic success.

❖ Opening hours: 6:30a.m. to 6:30p.m. daily

❖ Entrance fee: Free

2. Kyushu National Museum

As one of the national museums in Japan, its structure is striking and the exhibits are excellent with English signage.

❖ Opening hours: 9:30a.m. - 5p.m. (Sun, Tue - Thurs), 9:30a.m. - 8p.m. (Fri - Sat)

❖ Entrance fee: Adults - 430 yen, Students - 130 yen

3. Komyozen-ji

A Zen garden that is peaceful and a great place to escape from the crowds.

❖ Opening hours: 9:30a.m. - 4:30p.m. daily

❖ Entrance fee: 200 yen

Bonus Tip: It is advisable to visit there in the early morning or in the late evening during weekdays to avoid the crowds.

Kurokawa Onsen

Kurokawa Onsen is an attractive hot spring town filled with ryokan, public bath houses, attractive shops and cafes, a small shrine and bridges. It is where you should go if you are new to ryokan and want to experience what an onsen ryokan getaway is all about.

Tegata, a wooden pass, is sold for 1300 yen, providing admission to the baths of three different ryokan of one's choice. It is available at the information center and the participating ryokan.

Some of the famous baths here are Yamamizuki, Kurokawa-so and Shimmei-kan, with cave baths and riverside *rotemburo* (outdoor baths). There are mixed baths and women-only baths offered.

The town center is small and can be easily reached by foot. If you choose to stay at some of the more remote ryokan like Yamamizuki and Hozantei, pick-up service is usually provided. These ryokans also provide shuttle service. You can check the schedule at the information center.

* How to get there:

Kurokawa Onsen is not connected by train. A direct highway bus runs twice per day from Fukuoka Hakata Station to the place. (2.5 hours, 3090 yen).

Bonus Tip: Visit here during weekdays if possible. Do note that the shops here close early, so consider ryokan meals if you stay overnight.

Saga Pottery

There are a large number of kilns in Japan, each with its own unique type of products that reflect local culture and history. Arita, Imari and Karatsu are the three villages in Saga that are famous for their pottery. You would not want to miss Onta Village as well if you are into traditional Japanese ceramics ware.

1. Arita

The town of Arita is where Arita ware is produced. You can see chimneys of kilns all over the peaceful town. To learn about its history, pay a visit to the Kyushu Ceramics Museum and the Arita Ceramic Art Museum. Then, take a stroll along the special Tonbai Wall alleys and visit the local Sueyama Shrine.

The Wholesale Ceramics Plaza in Arita is the best for shopping as most items are discounted. If you like modern design, then you should visit the Kihara shop, which takes about a 10-minute walk from the Arita train station.

❖ How to get there: At Fukuoka's Hakata Station, take direct JR Midori and JR Huis Ten Bosch limited express trains (once per hour, 90 minutes, 3000yen) to get to Arita Station. The cost can be covered by the JR Pass and Kyushu Rail Pass.

Bonus Tip: Do note that many of Arita's main attractions are located around Kami-Arita Station. To get there directly, you have to take Hizen-Yamguchi limited express train (45 minutes) and transfer to a local train (35 minutes).

2. Imari

The town is famed with its porcelain and Imari wagyu steak. The Okawachiyama village nearby is also one of the main attractions. You can see the porcelain makers at work, and you can buy their products right there in the shops of the kilns.

❖ How to get there: Take a highway bus from Hakata Station in Fukuoka (1 hour 40 minutes). You can take a bus, or a taxi to go to Okawachiyama at Imari Station. Arita Station and Imari Station are connected by the Matsuura Railway (25 minutes, 460-yen one way, not covered by JR passes).

3. Karatsu

Karatsu ware is crafted to look most beautiful when food is presented on it. Its simplistic style has been especially prized in the world of the tea ceremony since ancient times.

Other than that, Karatsu Castle here offers beautiful views over Saga's northern coastline.

There are many restaurants that serve meals presented on Karatsu ware. Kawashima Tofu Shop is especially popular for their hand-made *zarudofu* (tofu served on a bamboo basket).

❖ How to get there: Go to Karatsu Station from Hakata Station (90 minutes, 1140 yen). The JR Pass is valid between Meinohama Station and Karatsu, but not on the subway line section. Rail pass holders need to pay an additional 300 yen from Hakata Station.

4. Onta Village

Onta ware is produced using traditional methods for over 300 years. There are only ten pottery studios as the number of studios is restricted to preserve the traditional production methods.

Wander around the serene village and delight in this secluded spot, picking up some earthy folk ware. Every family pottery has its own store. Every piece is handmade and unique.

❖ How to get there: Driving is the best option. Otherwise, take a taxi from Hita. Refer to this for more information: https://www.jnto.go.jp/eng/location/rtg/pdf/pg-806.pdf

Takachiho Gorge

This place is a real natural wonder. Old volcanic eruptions of Mount Aso carved a lave stream as deep as 80m to 100m through the rocks, and now water flows along the cracks. This gorge has stunning views with the vivid greenery in early summer and the tinted leaves in autumn.

You can choose to take in the impressive views of the gorge by hiking up the 1-km mountain trail, or taking a boat ride. You can rent boats at the south end of the gorge, and it is highly recommended to do so. The water is generally calm, and the view of the waterfalls from the boat is magnificent.

The Takachiho area is also the home to a number of wonderful shrines. Some of the popular ones are Takachiho Shrine and Amano-Iwato Shrine, where you can see Amano-Yasugawara that is said to have been the gathering place of many gods. You can also opt to buy a ticket (700 yen) and see a traditional Yokagura folk dance performance at 8p.m. every evening at the Kaguraden performance hall of Takachiho Shrine.

The restaurants around here offer good food too. Try the freshly made *somen nagashi* (bamboo float noodles).

❖ How to get there:

It takes a 30-40-minute walk to reach there from the Takachiho Bus Center. An infrequent tourist bus connects the gorge and the bus center and other tourist attractions on weekends and public holidays only.

There is also a direct bus that runs from JR Hakata Station to Takachiho Gorge (approximately 3 hours 45 minutes, 4020 yen one-way).

❖ Fee:

Boat Rental - 2000 yen per 30-min boat rental (max. 3 people)
Shrine Grounds - Free

❖ Opening Hours:

Boat Rental - 8:30a.m. to 5p.m.
Shrine Office - 8:30a.m. to 5p.m.

Suizenji Garden

Also known as Suizenji Jojuen Park, this beautiful and peaceful garden is specially designed such that its landscape represents the miniature of 53 post stations along the old highway, Tokaido Road that connected Edo (Tokyo) to Kyoto, and also includes a small Mount Fuji.

There are two shrines within the grounds of the park, namely Izumi Shrine and Inari Shrine. There is also an ancient Noh theatre that holds performances in the spring and autumn.

The building near the entrance of the park has its own story and is now used as a tearoom. For 650yen, you can enter the open-sided tatami room and enjoy a bowl of matcha tea and a Japanese sweet, while taking in the beautiful lakeside panorama.

❖ Opening hours:

7:30a.m. to 6p.m. (March to October) (last admission at 5:30p.m.)
8:30a.m. to 5p.m (November to February) (last admission at
4:30p.m.)

❖ Entrance fee:

Adults - 400yen, Children (age 6 - 15) - 200 yen

❖ How to get there:

It takes a 30-minute tram ride from JR Kumamoto Station to the
Suizenji Koen tram stop. Alternatively, take a train on the JR Hohi
Line to Shin-Suizenji Station, where you can walk to the garden
within 5 to 10 minutes.

Nagasaki

It is known for its horrific destruction caused by the atomic bomb
dropped during the World War II, but Nagasaki has been rebuilt and
is now a bustling city.

Places that you should pay a visit:

1. Nagasaki's Atomic Bomb Museum and Peace Memorial Hall

They serve as important places of cultural understanding. There are plenty of artefacts that remind people of the horror of wars and the importance of peace.

❖ Opening hours: 8a.m. - 5:30p.m. daily (September - April)
8a.m. - 6:30p.m. daily (May - August)

❖ Entrance fee: 200 yen (Museum)

❖ How to get there: A 4-minute walk from Matsuyama-machi Tram Station. Take a blue street car from Nagasaki Station to reach the museum.

2. Glover Garden

Glover Garden is an open-air museum that was once an area of foreigners' settlements. There are plenty of beautiful houses of former British and Scottish merchants. The garden's name is taken from the trader, Thomas Blake Glover, who began green tea commerce with Japan and lived his entire life there.

❖ Opening hours: 8a.m. - 6p.m. daily

❖ Entrance fee: Adults - 610-yen, High school student - 300 yen, Middle and elementary school student - 180 yen

❖ How to get there: A 5-minute walk from Oura Tenshudo-Shita Station.

3. Oura Catholic Church

Nagasaki was once the headquarters of missionary work in Japan. However, the Christians were later persecuted for 250 years. Christianity eventually revived there after a long and desperate underground period. Visit Oura Catholic Church that has been recently designated as UNESCO World Heritage to know about the grueling yet appealing history.

❖ Opening hours: 8a.m. - 6p.m. daily

❖ Entrance fee: 300 yen

❖ How to get there: A 5-minute walk from Oura Tenshudo-Shita Station. The entrance is just next to Glover Garden.

4. Dejima Museum

Don't miss out on this museum if you come to Nagasaki for its historical value. This Dutch trading post was once the only legal foreign presence in Japan. With detailed exhibits with excellent English signage, you will have a fruitful learning experience here. There is a kimono rental shop as well for those who want to feel even more in character.

❖ Opening hours: 8a.m. - 6p.m.

❖ Entrance fee: 510 yen

❖ How to get there: It is only a short walk from Dejima Station.

5. Inasayama

Mount Inasa (Inasayama) is a 333-meter high mountain that is near to Nagasaki's city center. Take a cable car in the evening to go up and enjoy the night views from the summit, which are ranked among Japan's three best night views.

❖ Operation hours: 9a.m. - 10p.m. (Gondolas depart every 15-20 minutes)

❖ Cable car fee: 1230 yen (round trip)/740 yen (one-way)

❖ How to get there: Take bus number 3 or 4 from Nagasaki Station (5 minutes, 150 yen) to go to Fuchi Shrine. Follow the crowd and pass through the shrine to find the ropeway station. Note that you should take bus number 20 or 40 from the opposite bus stop for the return trip.

Bonus Tip: If you happen to be in Nagasaki from Jan 1 to 15 of the Chinese Lunar Calendar, that is 5-9 Feb 2019, go to Nagasaki Shinchi Chinatown to view the famed Nagasaki Lantern Festival. During this time, similar to the Lantern Festival in China, over 15,000 lanterns brightly illuminate the city.

Amakusa

The islands of Amakusa have scenic nature, bountiful marine treasures and a fascinating history relating to Christianity.

These islands have plentiful beaches, hot springs and marine activities such as fishing, scuba, snorkeling and so on. Cherry blossom season (Mar/April) and the warm summer months (Oct/Nov) are the best times to visit for water activities.

As it is near to Nagasaki, where foreign missionaries first arrived in Japan, Amakusa became one of the main centers of evangelism. In the gruesome event, Shimabara Rebellion in 1637, thousands of Christians were persecuted. The rebellious leader, Amakusa Shiro, who was sixteen years old at that time, is remembered as a hero.

Top places to visit:

1. Sakitsu Cathedral Church

The church served as the center of Christianity in Amakusa during the mid-16th century. Standing in the middle of a small, calm fishing village, the Gothic-looking church makes for an unusual sight. Take some time to wander around the quaint village too. If you wish to visit here, you should give prior notice through this website: http://kyoukaigun.jp/en/visit/sakitsu.php

- ❖ Opening hours: 9a.m. - 5p.m. (Mon - Sat), 9:30a.m. - 5p.m. (Sun)

- ❖ Entrance fee: Free

- ❖ How to get there:

Driving there is recommended. Otherwise, refer to this brochure for access: http://kyoukaigun.jp/pdf/Amakusa_Eng.pdf

Bonus Tip: If you want to snorkel, stay in Sakitsu on the harbor at the Minato-ya. Wake up early to watch the sea mist lift with the church as a backdrop.

2. Oe Catholic Church

A beautiful church on top of a small hill that has been through the Edo period. After the Christianity ban was lifted in Meiji period, a French missionary nicknamed 'Pateru-san' and his followers completed the existing building together. Amakusa Rosario Museum is located at the bottom of the hill, where you can see the items related to the hidden Christians during the ban.

❖ Opening hours: 9a.m. - 5p.m. daily

❖ Entrance fee: Free

❖ Address: 1782 Amakusamachi Oe, Amakusa-shi

❖ How to get there: Driving there is recommended. Otherwise, take a taxi.

3. Amakusa Shiro Museum

The museum covers the Shimabara Rebellion with a focus on its young leader, Amakusa Shiro. A detailed English pamphlet and audio guide is available. There is also a meditation hall that allows people to meditate at the end of the journey.

❖ Opening hours: 9a.m. - 5p.m. daily except the second Tuesday of Jan and Jun (last admission at 4:20p.m.)

❖ Entrance fee: 600 yen

❖ Address: 977-1 Oyanomachinaka, Kamiamakusa 869-3603

❖ How to get there: Driving is the best option. Otherwise, take a taxi.

Bonus Tip: In April, you can join the Ushibuka Haiya Festival, which is a major spring event in which thousands of people dance through the streets to traditional folk songs.

Sakurajima

Sakurajima is a volcanic island that floats in the sea. It is one of the world's most active volcanoes and the symbol of Kagoshima. Sakurajima is the area's most prominent geographic feature as it is situated in the middle of Kagoshima Bay.

Sakurajiam has three main peaks: Kita-dake, Naka-dake and Minami-dake. Yunohira lookout is located midway up the mountain where eruptions can be observed. The volcano is most easily accessed by ferry.

Around the ferry terminal, you can have quite a number of activities. You may walk the Nagisa Lava Trail, which cuts through a lava zone created by the giant eruption in 1914. You can also opt for Nagisa Park Foot Bath, which is free of charge and a great place to take a break as well as to observe the volcano.

❖ How to get there:

Kagoshima and Sakurashima are connected by frequent ferries (15 minutes, 160 yen one-way). The ferry terminal is a ten-minute walk from JR Kagoshima Station or a five-minute walk from the Suizokukan-guchi tram stop.

❖ How to get around Sakurajima:

The easiest way is to travel by rental car, which can be taken onto the ferry (1150 yen one-way). Driving once around the coast takes about one hour.

There is a loop bus for tourists, the Sakurajima Island View Bus, that operates hourly from the ferry terminal to the Yunohira observation point and back. A one-day pass costs 500 yen.

Shiratani Unsuikyo Valley on Yakushima Island

Located at the south of Kagoshima, Yakushima is the rainiest place in Japan and hosts a unique ecosystem. Listed as one of the UNESCO sites, Yakushima is nature's paradise. You should stay here for at least one night to experience what the island has to offer.

Shirantani Unsuikyo Valley transports you to the settings of Hayao Miyazaki's Princess Mononoke; magical forests and waterfalls, fog and mist with plenty of greenery. There are 3 courses to choose from, ranging from 1 hour to 5 hours.

❖ How to get there:

Take a bus at Miyanoura Station that heads to Shiratani Unsui-kyo Valley (30 minutes, 550 yen)

❖ Note:

300-yen donation for the maintenance of the forest (optional)

Bonus Tips:

1. Many local buses stop running in winter due to the snow fall, so do pay attention to the bus schedule.

2. Due to the rainy, sub-tropical climate, it is advised to always check for the latest news.

3. It is very easy to get lost in the lush forest, so to enjoy your hike to the fullest, it is recommended to hire a guide.

4. Things to bring:

a) Quick-drying clothes

b) Rain gear

c) Plastic bags to seal your cellphone and clothes

d) Water-proof sports shoes

e) Hiking boots

f) Gloves

g) Hiking sticks

Chapter 9 - The Ultimate Japan Itineraries

I have created several itineraries during my tenure as a tourist guide in Japan. I have poured all my experience as a tourist guide to create these itineraries.

Generally, the most suitable months to go to Japan are March to May (late spring) and September to November (autumn).

You should travel around Japan by train. It is recommended to purchase a 7-day Japan Rail Pass as it is the most economical and worry-free way. Take note that you have to purchase it before entering the country.

Checklist

- ✓ Purchase a Japan Rail Pass if you are going to visit a lot of prefectures.

- ✓ Obtain an international license if you plan to drive.

- ✓ Book the tickets for performances or sumo tournaments and for Tokyo's Ghibli Museum, if you plan to visit there.

- ✓ Check online for local events that you might be interested in.

- ✓ Look for and rent a pocket wi-fi device.

- ✓ Master some basic Japanese phrases.

The Ultimate 7-Day Itinerary

Day 1: Tokyo

After you have arrived in Tokyo, check in to your hotel. Rest for a while and visit one of the world's most populated cities.

Go to Harajuku and visit the Meiji Jingu shrine. Explore the shrine for about an hour. Take as many pictures as you like. You can visit Takeshita Street after that. Next, go straight to the Imperial Palace and experience the royal garden for real.

Take the Ginza subway to Shibuya station. Stand next to the Hachiko Statue and take some photos. Then, cross the famous crossing. You can have lunch in the area. You could visit the Parco Museum and the Bankamura Museum of Art. You can eat ramen in Ichiran and sushi in Umegaoka Sushi No Midori Sohonten. If you want some Italian food, you may want to check out La Bisboccia.

From Shibuya, go to the station on JR Yamanote line and take a train to Tokyo Tower. Be sure to visit Sensoji Temple on your way back. After two hours, take a train to Roppongi and eat dinner there. You can try out the elegant restaurants such as Ryugin, Takazawa, Narazawa, and Jomon Roppongi. You can also visit cocktail bars in the area if you want to enjoy the Tokyo nightlife.

Day 2 and Day 3: Mount Fuji and Lake Kawaguchi

Visit Lake Kawaguchi. Once you have arrived there, check in a local ryokan and start exploring the lake. Every second count! You can take the red and green line on the first day and the blue line on the second day. The blue line is much longer. It only has one bus every hour. If you get a sightseeing bus pass, it will be worth the money if you visit 3 places of interest or more in one day.

Day 4: Kyoto

Spend the day in Kyoto. You can join day tours. However, you can also take trains and buses to popular destinations on your own. Here is my recommendation when it comes to Kyoto:

- Arashiyama Bamboo Grove. Go there early in the morning or late in the evening on weekdays.

- Kinkaku-ji (The Golden Pavilion)

- Lunch

- Kiyomizu-dera Temple

- Fushimi-Inari-Taisha Shrine

- The Nishiki Market (Dinner)

- Rest

Day 5: Nara

Take a train to Nara the first thing in the morning. You will need one whole day for Nara. It is time to feed the deer and witness the greatness of the Todaiji temple. Below is a list of how you should visit Nara for maximum experience in the shortest time.

- Nara Deer Park

- Todaiji Temple

- Kasuga-taisha Shrine

- Yoshikien

Day 6: Osaka

Visit the famous Osaka castle and the Dotonbori district. You should also check out the Instant Ramen Museum and Kuromon Ichiba Market. If you have more time, you can visit the Universal Studio in Osaka.

Day 7: Fly out

You may have to take the train back to Tokyo in order to fly back home or fly out from Osaka on the 7th day. However, if you have more time, you can make your way back to Tokyo as early as possible. After that, you can spend some time shopping once you have arrived at the Tokyo station. Do note that you can use your JR Pass to take the Narita Express, or the Tokyo Monorail to Haneda airport for free.

The Extended Version: 10-Day Itinerary

If you have a few more days there, you can choose to go to the places mentioned in the 7-day itinerary at a slower pace, or refer to the following itinerary.

- Day 1 - Arrive in Tokyo
- Day 2 - Explore Tokyo
- Day 3 - Disneysea/Disneyland
- Day 4 - Go to Mount Fuji and Lake Kawaguchi. Staying in an onsen is highly recommended.
- Day 5 - Explore Mount Fuji/Hakone region
- Day 6 - Depart to Kyoto. Explore Kyoto. You can have a Gion evening tour.
- Day 7 - Explore Kyoto
- Day 8 - Day trip to Nara
- Day 9 - Depart to Osaka. Explore Osaka.
- Day 10 - Fly out

7 Days in Tokyo and Hokkaido

Hokkaido is one of the most beautiful islands in Japan. It has interesting landscapes and captivating sceneries. Here's a 7-day Tokyo and Hokkaido itinerary:

Day 1: Tokyo and Mount Fuji

After you have arrived in Tokyo, go to your hotel and take a short rest. Then, take a bus to Fujisan Fifth Station (Mt. Fuji). The trip takes about two hours. Once you have arrived at the station, you can enjoy the fascinating view of the mountain. You can also visit the Shiraito falls as a side trip after that. Eat dinner at a nearby restaurant and then head back to Tokyo.

Day 2: Tokyo

Go to Tsukiji Market early in the morning. Then, take a train to Chiyoda Ward and explore the beautiful Imperial Palace Park in Chiyoda Ward. It's a peaceful and serene royal park filled with cherry trees.

Next, if you're into shopping, make sure to explore the streets of Ginza, Shibuya and Harajuku. You could find a lot of posh stores in Shibuya. And if you're into cosplay, you'll definitely love Harajuku. You can eat lunch in Shibuya after that.

After your lunch, visit the great Tokyo Tower and Tokyo Skytree in Asakusa. Take your dinner around Asakusa area.

After dinner, take a night train to Shin-Hakodate-Hokuto. The trip takes about four hours.

Once you arrive at Shin-Hakodate-Hokuto station, take a train to Sapporo. This trip takes 7 hours and 30 minutes. You can simply sleep on the train. Many travelers do that to save time and money. You can also get there by flight which will be much faster.

Day 3: Sapporo

Check in your hotel. Then, go to see the famous landmarks in the city – the TV tower in Odori Park and the former government office. Then, have your lunch around the area.

After lunch time, get some booze at the Sapporo Beer Museum. Don't forget to explore the Sapporo Beer Garden as well. Then, eat the authentic Sapporo ramen for dinner.

After dinner, take a train (Toho Line) to Odori Station. Then, ride a bus to the Moiwa Fumoto Station and walk to the peak of Mount Moiwa. This mountain gives you an excellent city view. You can also ring the bell of happiness to attract true love.

Day 4: Otaru

Otaru is one of the most beautiful old cities that you'll ever see in your lifetime. Take a train from Sapporo to Otaru (the trip takes about 45 minutes). Don't forget to visit the Otaru Canal. Then, visit the Music Box Museum on Saikamachi Dori Street. Take time to explore the Sankaku Fish Market to get delicious sushi. You can have lunch and dinner in various restaurants such as Mazasushi, Kamaei, and Takarasushi. After dinner, head back to Sapporo.

Day 5: Furano

Spend the whole day in Furano. Take a bus from Sapporo to Nakafurano. You can walk from Nakafurano to Farm Tomita, or you can take a taxi. Take your lunch at Farm Tomita.

Next, get to the Municipal Lavender Field and enjoy the purple carpet.

Depart for Biei in the evening. Then, have your dinner and settle down at your hotel.

Day 6: Biei

After taking your breakfast, visit the tourist information center near Biei Station. Get on your bus, sit back and enjoy the whole journey. It is recommended for you to join two courses: one in the morning, and another one in the afternoon. The sightseeing bus will bring you to all the top destinations in Biei.

Day 7: Fly out

You can explore Sapporo a little bit more and visit the malls. Then, fly out from Sapporo New Chitose Airport (CTS-New Chitose).

3 Days in Tokyo for Food Hunters

Day 1

Hamarikyu Gardens - Asakusa - Tokyo Skytree - Shinatatsu Ramen Street

From Shinagawa Station, go to Hamamatsucho Station and walk to Hamarikyu Gardens. Participate in the low-key, do-it-yourself tea ceremony at the tea house there. For about 500 yen, you will be provided with a cup of matcha, a traditional *wagashi* (Japanese sweet) and a guide on how a tea ceremony is performed.

Then, take a water bus on the Sumida River to Asakusa. It takes around 40 minutes. There are other ways to get there, but this is a fun way to get a different view of the city. In Asakusa, there are lots of choices for lunch. Try out Tempura Daikokuya. They don't accept credit cards, so make sure that you have cash.

After that, head to the Tokyo Skytree, which is located at a twenty-minute walk away from Asakusa. You can also take the TOBU Skytree line to go there. If you want to skip the line, you can purchase the slightly more expensive ticket (extra 1000yen) for foreigners that allows you to bypass the line.

Go to Shinagawa and visit Shinatatsu Ramen Street to have dinner. There are 7 ramen shops and a few other restaurants that serve various things. You can try a couple of different ramen that you like.

Day 2

Tsukiji Fish Market - Shibuya - Tokyo Food Show -

Kurand Sake Market (optional) - Meiji Jingu Shrine - Harajuku

Head to Tsukiji Outer Market. Book a tour of the market, or enjoy strolling around the market yourself. Have a delicious sushi meal here!

Then, take the Ginza line to Shibuya and experience the famous Shibuya crossing. Once you have done the shopping, head to the Tokyo Food Show in the Shibuya station. This is the perfect spot to see and taste the wide variety of Japanese food.

If you want to try sake, go to Kurand Sake Market nearby to sample over 100 varieties of sake from different breweries. You can bring your own snacks and bites. For about 3000 yen, you are free to sample as much sake as you like with no time limit.

After having your lunch, visit the Meiji Jingu Shrine in the vicinity.

After learning a bit of the history, you can head back to the Harajuku area and have some snacks. You can find all kinds of shops and restaurants providing a variety of food.

Day 3

Atre Department Store - Tokyo Station - Ramen Street -

Imperial Palace East Gardens – Ueno

Head to Atre Department Store in Shinagawa to have a delicious sushi breakfast. Then, explore the Tokyo Station, which is like a mini city itself. As a food lover, you should visit Kitchen Street and Japan Gourmet Street. Gransta Marunouchi, a shopping center, is just outside the train station too.

For lunch, go to the Ramen street in the station. There are 8 vendors here and you can choose whichever you like.

After the meal, make a quick stop at Tokyo Okashi Land to check out the unique Japanese snacks, especially if you're looking for something to take back as gifts for family and friends.

Then, visit the Imperial Palace East Gardens. It's about a 10-minute walk from the Tokyo Station.

Have dinner in the Ueno area. You can choose to have a food tour here or walk around on your own. The street food there is popular and budget-friendly.

5 Days in Kyushu

Day 1

Fukuoka

As you arrived in Fukuoka, check in your hotel, and spend a day in Fukuoka. Buy the Kyushu Rail Pass if you are going to take public transport.

Day 2

Pottery Towns and Kurokawa Onsen

Rent a car in Fukuoka and drive to the pottery towns. Choose the ones that you like. Refresh at the restaurant nearby and head to Kurokawa Onsen. Buy the ticket and visit up to 3 *rotembuto*. Then, stay a night there.

Day 3

Aso-san and Kumamoto

After breakfast, head to Aso-san and enjoy the views. Take your lunch here as well. Then, drive to Kumamoto. Though the castle is under renovation, you can still walk around the grounds and talk a stroll at Suzenji Park. Try *basashi* here.

Day 4

Sakurajima, Nagasaki and Amakusa

Go to Kagoshima for the famous Sakurajima. Walk around and have lunch here. After that, drive to Nagasaki and take the ferry ride to Amakusa. Visit Sakitsu Cathedral Church and Oe Cathedral Church. Press on and take the ferry to go back to Nagasaki. Have your dinner at the China town and explore the Glover Garden. At night, go up Inasayama by cable car.

Day 5

Nagasaki and fly out

Explore more of the city of Nagasaki. Alternatively, drive to one of the pottery towns that you have missed. Go back to Fukuoka and fly out.

If you have a couple of days to spare, go to the magical Yakushima for some hiking.

Practical Tips

➤ Cash is important. Some smaller businesses won't take credit cards.

➤ If you have tattoos, consider keeping yourself reasonably covered up as tattoos are still frowned upon in public.

➤ Avoid the first week of May, when the 'Golden Week' holidays result in packed trains, jammed roads and crowds.

➤ Meals at lunch time can be a whole lot cheaper.

➤ Prepare slip-on shoes as you will be taking off your shoes a lot.

Chapter 10 - 50 Japan Travel and Budget Tips

As a seasoned tourist guide in Japan, I have compiled the budget and travel tips that you can use while touring Japan:

1. Buy discounted rail tickets in stores called "kinken" shops. These stores also sell discounted concert tickets and gift certificates.

2. Use the local buses. This will allow you to enjoy the scenery. Bus fares are cheap, too.

3. If you have a lot of time, try biking around the city. You can also just walk around.

4. Try self-serve udon (noodle) restaurants.

5. If you have a big appetite, you could go for the "eat all you can" restaurants.

6. Visit the local bakeries to try sweetbreads.

7. Stay at a capsule hotel, or a guest house.

8. If you're really on a budget, you can try couchsurfing, which is totally free!

9. Always bring an umbrella.

10. Learn common words like "arigato" or thank you, "hai" or yes, "gomennasai" or sorry, and "dozo" or please.

11. If you're traveling with family, it's best to use Airbnb.

12. You can also sleep in Onsen and Karaoke Rooms.

13. You can also stay in a temple.

14. Go to 100-yen shops to score incredible discounts, the most popular one will be Daiso, and trust me it is big.

15. Go to flea markets.

16. Travel to Japan during the bargain period which usually happens during the Chinese New Year.

17. Do your laundry in coin Laundromats.

18. Make sure that you have back-up copies of your travel documents – passport and visa.

19. Use disposable underwear.

20. Plan your outfits ahead.

21. Stay hydrated.

22. Make sure that you save your hotel phone number and address on your phone.

23. Japan is also the land of hackers. So, avoid public Wi-Fi services.

24. Be respectful of Japan's customs.

25. Opt for free tourist spots.

26. Cash is the most popular mode of payment in Japan, so make sure you have enough yen.

27. Buy a local rail pass. You can also buy a regional rail pass if you plan to travel from one city to another.

28. Trains in Japan do not operate 24/7. Train stations close at 1 am.

29. Tattoos are taboo in Japan (only the members of the Yakuza gang have visible tattoos). So, make sure to cover your tattoo if you can.

30. Japanese people love American culture. So, don't be shock if Tokyo looks a lot like New York.

31. You do not have to give tips.

32. Don't raise your hand to call the waiter. You can simply use the buzzer.

33. Bow when you meet someone new.

34. Take your shoes off when going to a temple.

35. Wash your hands before you enter a shrine.

36. Don't be afraid to ask for help from locals.

37. Don't miss the nightlife in Tokyo or Osaka.

38. Pack light.

39. Use the takuhaibin or the luggage forwarding services.

40. Use your own Wi-Fi device.

41. You should carry earthquake survival kits.

42. Avoid taxis when you can because they are expensive.

43. Do not take photos in restricted areas like temples and castles.

44. Make a hotel reservation.

45. Check the weather forecast in Japan.

46. Bring your prescribed medicines.

47. Do not be afraid to be adventurous.

48. Do not use chopsticks to pass food.

49. You can shop in train stations.

50. Do not stab your food using your chopsticks.

Japan's Secrets and Weirdness: What's So Special About Japan?

Japan is the land of the mystical ninjas and the graceful geishas. It's the home of animes and everything cute. But, what is Japan's secret? What makes it stand out from all other countries? What makes Japan, Japan?

Well here are seventy (70) reasons why Japan is unique and different from other countries:

1. Its advance technology.

2. The beautiful cherry blossoms.

3. The short haiku poetry.

4. You could wear Kimono while walking around the busy city of Tokyo.

5. Taxis that automatically open.

6. KFC meals for Christmas.

7. Free tissues as part of their advertising campaign.

8. You could find love hotels everywhere and they come with costumes.

9. Clean tap water, and yes, even the tap water in the toilet.

10. It's the largest car manufacturer in the world.

11. The Japanese customer service is the best in the world.

12. Japanese people always strive for excellence.

13. Japanese people have superior manners. They bow to people they meet.

14. Electronic bidets.

15. Touchscreen menus.

16. The buses are always on time.

17. It has more than three thousand McDonald's stores.

18. Japan celebrates the penis every spring time in an event called "The Steel Phallus Festival".

19. Vending machines sell just about anything from snacks to umbrellas, women's underwear, and even porn.

20. KitKat comes in different flavors like corn and grapes.

21. The Japanese consider black cats as a sign of good fortune.

22. The Japanese people have a strict code of honor. Defeated Japanese warriors perform Harakiri, or honor suicide. They'd rather die than lose face.

23. Japan went through a lot. Its cities were once destroyed during the Second World War.

24. Japan's unemployment rate is only four percent.

25. The beers in vending machines are cheap.

26. You can drink beer anywhere. But, you're not allowed to eat while walking.

27. The Japanese bullet trains are some of the fastest in the world.

28. You could stay in capsule hotels for less than $20 a night.

29. You could find katana blades (Samurai sword) in museums.

30. The internet in Japan is really fast.

31. Desserts are wrapped in delicate and colorful papers.

32. The bridges in Japan are beautiful.

33. You could find unique toilet ikebanas.

34. Mayonnaise is not for sandwiches in Japan. It is used for noodles, pancakes, potato chips, and ice cream.

35. Japanese sometimes use full body umbrellas.

36. Japan has weird ice cream flavors – octopus, charcoal, cactus, and horse meat.

37. Japanese people allow their children to clean the house using baby mops.

38. Malls have short escalators.

39. The country has a suicide forest located at the base of Mount Fuji.

40. Japanese people are obsessed with comics.

41. Japanese people have a long life. In fact, there are more than fifty thousand people in Japan that are more than one hundred years old.

42. The Japanese people say sorry in twenty different ways.

43. Japan is the home of the longest running company in the world.

44. It has six thousand and eight hundred islands.

45. The average delay of trains in Japan is eighteen seconds.

46. There are more pet dogs and cats than children.

47. Most of the mobile phones in Japan are waterproof.

48. There's a lot of cat cafes in Japan where you could hang out and play with cats for hours.

49. Japan has more than five million vending machines.

50. Sleeping on the job is acceptable in Japan.

51. Teachers and students clean the classrooms and the school cafeteria.

52. More than five hundred kids in Japan fainted after a sad and dramatic Pokemon episode in 1997.

53. Japan has an island that's filled with rabbits.

54. Most streets in Japan do not have a name.

55. The Burger King in Japan has an all-black burger.

56. There's a Snoopy Museum in Japan.

57. The average lifespan of a Japanese person is 83 years.

58. In ancient Japan, samurais and Buddhist monks actually engage in homosexual relationships.

59. A village called Nagoro has more life-sized dolls than people.

60. A highway passes through a building.

61. You can't see homeless people in the streets. Most homeless people sleep in internet cafes.

62. Japan is one of the few Asian countries that were not colonized by Europe.

63. Karoshi is common in Japan. It means death caused by stress and working long hours.

64. Prisoners in the death row do not know when their execution is. So, they live each day like it's their last.

65. Bitcoin is a common mode of payment in Japan.

66. There's a museum for parasites.

67. You don't want to have a criminal case in Japan. It has a ninety-nine percent conviction rate.

68. Japan has square watermelons.

69. Because of the huge success of animes, there are more than one hundred voice acting schools in the country.

70. Some of their students go to two schools in one day, one in the morning and another one at night.

Japan is smaller than California. It was isolated for years and yet, it is one of the most intriguing superpowers of the world. It has three thousand McDonald's, and yet you could still find hundreds of old temples around the country.

What makes Japan special is its culture, people, fascinating landscapes, and rich history. It's a land like no other. It's a land of honor, respect, innovation, and raw beauty.

I believe that you should visit Japan at least once in your life. But, let me warn you- once is not going to be enough.

Conclusion

I hope that this book was able to help you plan for your trip to Japan.

✓ Japan is a beautiful place that has a strong Eastern charm. But, it's one of the most technologically advanced countries in the world, too.

✓ Be clear about how much you want to spend on a trip. This will help you pick the right tourist spots to visit. If you're on a budget, it's best to visit only two cities and opt for free tourist spots. But, if you have money to burn, stay in fancy hotels and hop from one island to another to enjoy everything that Japan has to offer.

✓ If you don't have a lot of time, it's best that you visit only Tokyo or Kyoto. You could also opt to visit Hokkaido.

✓ To maximize your time, it's a good idea to fly to one airport and fly out at another airport. For example, you can fly into the Osaka Airport and fly out from Tokyo.

✓ Plan your trip carefully.

✓ Do not buy an all-access pass unless you're sure that you really need it.

✓ Take overnight buses from one city to another. This will save you time and money.

✓ Travel slowly. Enjoy the sceneries and the views. Look out at the window when you're on a train or a bus.

✓ Don't be afraid to visit unpopular spots. These spots are beautiful, unique, and usually cheap.

Lastly, have fun. Japan is definitely one of the most beautiful and interesting countries in the world. I hope that you will enjoy your trip.

Maps & Resources

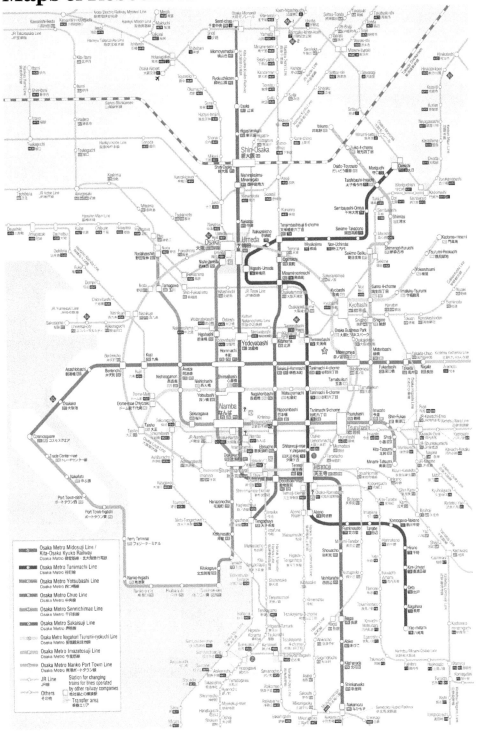

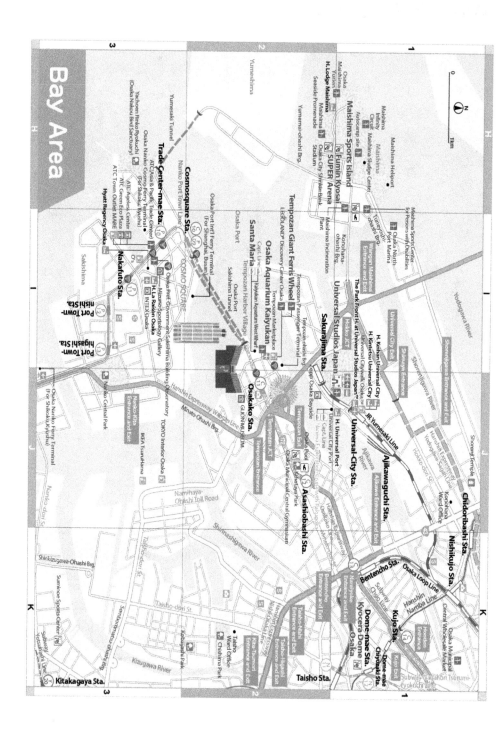

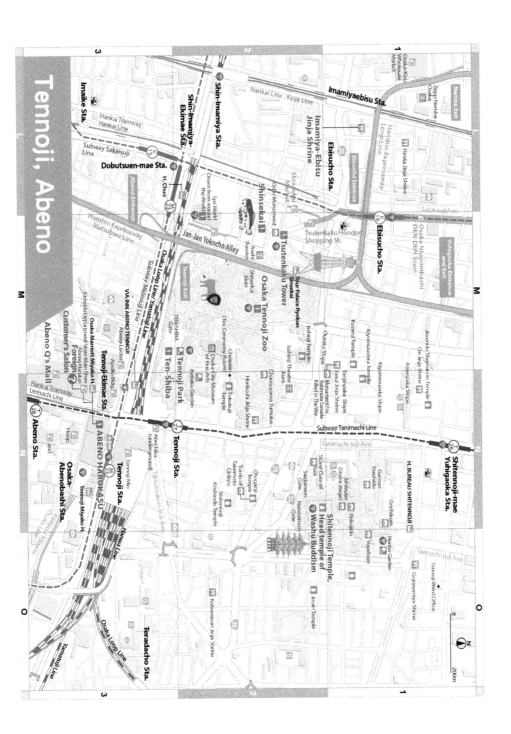

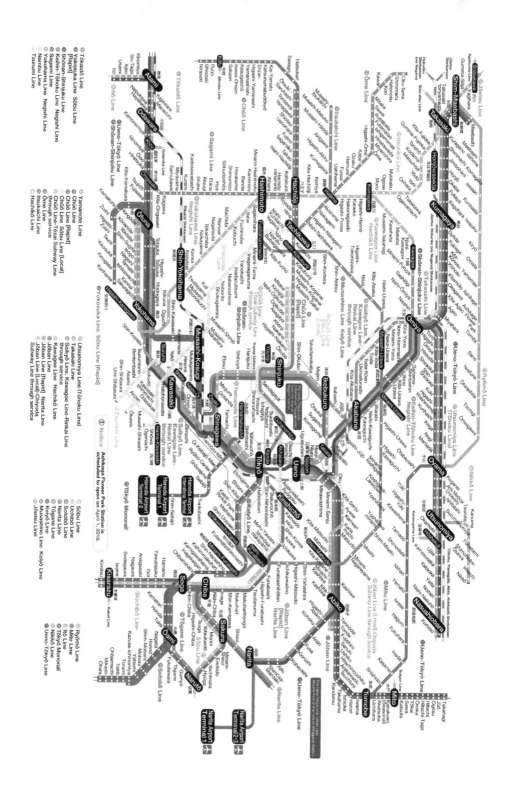